FRACTURED
GENERATIONS

CRAFTING A
FAMILY POLICY FOR
TWENTY-FIRST-CENTURY
AMERICA

FRACTURED GENERATIONS

ALLAN CARLSON

TRANSACTION PUBLISHERS
NEW BRUNSWICK (U.S.A.) AND LONDON (U.K.)

Copyright © 2005 by Transaction Publishers, New Brunswick, New Jersey.
www.transactionpub.com

All rights reserved under International and Pan-American Copyright Conventions. No part of this book may be reproduced or transmitted in any form or by any means, electronic or mechanical, including photocopy, recording, or any information storage and retrieval system, without prior permission in writing from the publisher. All inquiries should be addressed to Transaction Publishers, Rutgers—The State University, 35 Berrue Circle, Piscataway, New Jersey 08854-8042.

This book is printed on acid-free paper that meets the American National Standard for Permanence of Paper for Printed Library Materials.

Library of Congress Catalog Number: 2004051291
ISBN: 0-7658-0275-9
Printed in the United States of America

Library of Congress Cataloging-in-Publication Data

Carlson, Allan C.
    Fractured generations : crafting a family policy for twenty-first century
America / Allan Carlson.
        p. cm.
    Includes bibliographical references and index.
    ISBN 0-7658-0275-9 (alk. paper)
        1. Family—United States. 2. Family policy—United States. I. Title.

HQ536.C373   2005
306.85'0973—dc22

2004051291

*To All American Parents in
Natural Family Homes*

Contents

Introduction

Fifty years ago, the phrase "family policy" was rarely heard in America. Responding to plunging birthrates, the West European nations had constructed "population policies" during the 1920s and 1930s to stimulate fertility, but nothing of the sort happened here. Some form of "welfare policy," including social insurance and means-tested relief, was common by then to most industrial societies, including the United States. The American states also maintained laws governing marriage, divorce, education, inheritance, and child protection, which regulated the formation, childrearing practices, and dissolution of families. Moreover, the growing burden of income taxation required judgments regarding the treatment of marriage and children. Yet these scattered policy areas were rarely seen as closely related.

The primary reason for this, it seems, was actually the continued normative strength of the idea of "The American Family." Most Americans still knew in 1954 what "family" connoted: it meant marriage, householding, children, and care of the aged; it meant a bonding of the generations. The family, as such, was normal and natural, part of the expected course for each adult life.

The American past seemed to support this laissez faire view, as well. For example, the Founders rarely talked about "family" and the word is not found in the Constitution. Clearly, though, this was not because they cared too little for it; rather, family was so central to their lives as to barely need mention. Indeed, it is arguable that the American nation was unusually family-centric, from its colonial origins through the mid-twentieth-century baby boom.[1] Family policy as such could be deemed unnecessary, for it was quietly assumed by lawmakers and citizens alike that *all* policies would naturally be in favor of the family.

In practice, though, this assumption did not entirely hold up. As far back as the 1840s, state policies regarding the "common schools" and child protection were already contributing to a quiet weakening of families; certain "progressive" innovations in the early twentieth century (such as the idea of "the school as a substitute for the family") did so as well. Still, it was only during the 1960s that attacks on the family in America grew open and widespread. Equity feminists objected to a home economy resting on the "breadwinner/homemaker/three-child" model found in the burgeoning American suburbs, and assaulted its core institution: the family wage paid to fathers. Neo-Malthusians fretted over the healthy fertility numbers recorded during the 1950s and propagandized for "zero-" and then "negative-population growth." The sexual revolutionaries, ranging from slick publicists like Hugh Hefner to pseudoscientific "sexologists" at the Kinsey Institute, labored to sever the bonds between sex and marriage and sex and procreation. Militant secularists turned to the federal court system to challenge the place of religiously grounded morality in American public life.

These four ideological movements did score dramatic successes in their common campaign to disrupt American homes. The U.S. Supreme Court banned prayer in public schools in 1963, affirmed contraception as a right in 1968, did the same for abortion in 1973, devalued fathers' rights in 1976, and, most recently, crafted rights to sodomy and homosexuality (2003). Meanwhile, the U.S. Congress shifted the income tax burden away from the unmarried, the childless, and the mega-corporations, placing it instead on the backs of married couples with two or more children. Congress also gave rich new subsidies to parents using daycare; families with a parent full-time at home got nothing. For their part, federal regulators squelched the cultural assumptions that had sustained the family wage ideal.

These unprecedented political and legal challenges had results. The "marriage boom" and the "baby boom" of the 1940-64 era were replaced by the "baby bust" and the retreat from marriage that marked the next forty years. Marital fertility fell sharply while the divorce rate and out-of-wedlock birthrate soared. The elderly flowed into age-segregated housing and nursing homes. By the year 2000, the bonds of the generations were rent, or fractured, in America.

One lesson of history is clear: No nation can go forward, or even survive, without a durable family system. The family is the source of new life and the crucible of character that makes ordered liberty possible.[2] Contemporary family policy represents an attempt to counter the negative forces of the last four decades and to restore the natural family to its necessary place in American life.

As a foundation, effective family policy requires a normative definition of "the family" against which policy goals and results might be measured. In this book, the definition used comes from a preparatory session for the World Congress of Families II, held in May 1998. Gathering in a room dating back to the second century B.C. in the Eternal City of Rome, representatives from the world's nations and faiths (including this author) agreed that:

> The natural family is the fundamental social unit, inscribed in human nature, and centered around the voluntary union of a man and a woman in a lifelong covenant of marriage for the purposes of: satisfying the longings of the human heart to give and receive love; welcoming and ensuring the full physical and emotional development of children; sharing a home that serves as the center for social, educational, economic, and spiritual life; building strong bonds among the generations to pass on a way of life that has transcendent meaning; and extending a hand of compassion to individuals and households whose circumstances fall short of these ideals.

All healthy human societies rest on this common social form, which is rooted in turn in a shared human nature, an aspect of the Creation (ref. Genesis 1 and 2). It is true that around this universal definition, distinctive national qualities of family living also emerge. Even so, it is more accurate to refer to The Family in America (or, say, The Family in Canada or The Family in Kenya) rather than to The American Family. The former term correctly implies that each nation may be judged by the manner in which it treats the natural and universal human family unit. Put into shorthand, then, contemporary family policy should aim at securing the stability, the autonomy, and the fecundity of the natural family in America.

This book holds to that goal. The chapters began as a special "Family Policy" lecture series for policymakers and the public sponsored by the Family Research Council in Washington, DC, during the program year 2002/03. They offer a fresh look at critical issues facing the family in America and lay out new approaches to pro-family policy formation that are appropriate to conditions in the early twenty-first century.

In another sense, this book represents a sequel to *Family Questions: Reflections on the American Social Crisis*, first published in 1988. While using wholly new material, it explores some similar themes (e.g., population, housing policy, the nature of the suburb), and focuses on some common answers, including the value of "pro-family" tax reform.

In organization, the book follows the life-course of the human family: marriage; the birth of children; infant and toddler care;

schooling; building a home; crafting a durable family economy; and elder care. The first chapter examines the terrible assaults recently launched in this land against the ancient institution of marriage, and offers old/new ways to think about the marital bond. Chapter two dissects the failure of existing American policies affecting human fertility, at home and abroad, and proposes fresh strategies for a now "depopulating" world. The third chapter analyzes the failed promises and real damage caused by widespread, publicly subsidized non-parental care of infants and toddlers. The means to restore primary and secondary education of the young as vehicles for family strengthening, neighborhood building, and a true homecoming concern chapter four. The next chapter examines the strengths and weaknesses of the peculiar institution of the American suburb, and proposes ways to make this mode-of-life more family friendly. The powerful ability of the federal tax system to influence family formation and family health, for good and ill, is the focus of chapter six. The seventh chapter explores the broader nature of the family economy, and lays out ways to strengthen this necessary material base of the autonomous American home. Analysis of the mounting "elder care crisis" in America and ways to rebuild the multigenerational family occupy chapter eight. The volume concludes with a summary of policy proposals, a distinctively "American" family policy for the twenty-first century.

For the steady encouragement given to this project, I need to thank the good folk associated with the Family Research Council during the 2002/2003 season: Tony Perkins, Kenneth J. Connor, Colin Stewart, Alan Crippen II, Brian Robertson, Bridget Maher, Douglas Minson, Mark Haskew, Genevieve Wood, Peter Sprigg, Timothy Dailey, and Kristin Hansen. Through their support and advice, this book became a true collaborative effort. I also need thank Heidi Gee back in Rockford, Illinois, for her usual fine job in managing the word processing tasks.

Looking at the powerful forces now arrayed against the family in America, it would be easy to succumb to despair. I dedicate this book to those parents, everywhere in the country, who resist the formidable modern pressures placed on their families and who make the sacrifices necessary to craft strong and fruitful homes. All hope for the future of this nation lies with them.

Notes

1. My own efforts to document this statement can be found in: Allan Carlson, *The Family in America: Searching for Social Harmony in the Industrial Age* (New Brunswick, NJ: Transaction Publishers, 2003); and Allan Carlson, *The "American Way": Family and Community in the Shaping of the American Identity* (Wilmington, DE: ISI Books, 2003).
2. A solid affirmation of this statement may be found in: Carle Zimmerman, *Family and Civilization* (New York and London: Harper & Brothers, 1947).

1

Marriage on Trial

There is a curious dichotomy in American public life today. On the one hand, those who are able—and in many ways encouraged—to marry are in increasing numbers choosing *not* to do so. Overall, the U.S. marriage rate has fallen nearly 50 percent since 1960. The proportion of American women aged twenty-five to twenty-nine who have never married, slightly below 10 percent in 1965, reached 39 percent in 2000: a four-fold increase. Among men of the same ages, the increase in the never married category was from 18 percent in 1965 to 44.4 percent in 2000. What the Census Bureau now calls "*un*married partner households" have climbed in number from 523,000 cohabiting heterosexual couples in 1970 to 4,900,000 in 2000: a nine-fold increase. Meanwhile, the count of non-family households in America, with *neither* marriage nor children present, soared from a mere 7 million in 1960 to nearly 33 million in 2000: a figure over four times as great. At the same time, the number of married couple families with children actually declined slightly in absolute numbers, from 25.7 million back in 1960 to 25.2 million in 2000. Viewed proportionately, married couple families formed 76 percent of all households in 1960, but only 53 percent in 2000. We also see what University of Southern California sociologist Kingsley Davis calls a "Declining Marital Output"; that is, fewer children. The U.S. Marital Fertility Rate fell from 157 (births per 1000 Married Women, ages eighteen to forty-four) in 1957 to only eighty-four in 1995: a dramatic retreat from children.[1]

On the other hand, there is mounting clamor for access to legal marriage among persons in relationships traditionally denied such treatment. As Lambda Legal explains: "Same-sex couples want to get married for the same...reasons as any other couple: they seek security and protection that come from a legal union...; they want the recognition from family, friends and the outside world...; and they seek the structure and support for their emotional and economic bonds that a marriage provides."[2] Many legal analysts believe that the U.S. Supreme Court's 2003 decision in *Lawrence and Garner v. Texas* has opened the door to an affirmation of same-sex marriage.

There are broader legal challenges to the contemporary institution of marriage as well. A series of recommendations from the American Law Institute (ALI), issued in November 2002, would strip traditional marriage of most of its distinctive legal status: not by direct repeal, but rather by extending the protections afforded by marriage to other relationships. The proposals, for example, would extend alimony and property rights to cohabiting domestic partners, both hetero- and homosexual: "a domestic partner is entitled to compensatory payments on the same basis as a spouse." Moreover, the ALI urges that adultery be eliminated as a factor in deciding divorce issues such as child custody and the division of property: "Justice is hardly served by treating one spouse's adultery as relevant to the alimony inquiry." The number of persons who could claim custody of or visitation rights with a child would also expand, to include a "de facto parent" such as the lesbian partner of a child's biological mother.[3] Meanwhile, The Alliance for Marriage—chaired by former District of Columbia Delegate Walter Fauntroy—has put forward in this Congress a proposed Amendment to the U.S. Constitution declaring that "Marriage in the United States shall consist only of the union of a man and a woman" and prohibiting courts from conferring marital status on other couples or groups.

Looking at developments in all Western nations, two scholars note that legal structures touching on marriage that had been "fairly stable over several centuries have quite suddenly crumbled under the combined pressure of capitalism, individualism, and moral anomie." Where "marriage used to be for life," an exit through divorce has now become easy and unilateral. The legal role of marriage in conferring legitimacy on children has also been swept away. Informal partnerships have gained a rough equality with traditional marriage. "[E]ven one of the last remnants of traditional family law, the requirement that spouses and parents be of different gender, has come under siege," with some nations now extending "marriage-like rights to same gender couples." As the authors conclude: "The principles that uncontestedly dominated family law for hundreds of years have been turned topsy-turvy."[4]

It is also curious to note that, back in 1926, the new Communist rulers of Soviet Russia shocked the world with a plan to abolish the legal registration of marriage. As one of the measure's most passionate advocates, the public prosecutor Krilenko, explained:

> Why should the State know who marries whom? Of course, if living together and not registration is taken as the test of a married state, polygamy and polyandry may exist; but the State can't put up any barriers against this. Free love is the ultimate aim of a socialist state; in that State marriage will be free from any kind of obligation, including economic, and will turn into an absolutely free union of two beings.[5]

While Communism failed horribly and violently as an economic and political system, its social vision of marriage as "free from any kind of obligation, including economic" has actually been achieved in Western Europe, most completely in Sweden. There, the label "marriage" survives, but it confers no meaningful status. All social benefits and taxes assume that the married couple is actually two individuals. Moreover, a "traditional marriage" of breadwinner husband/homemaking wife actually pays a large financial penalty.[6] As the American Law Institute Report suggests, the legal profession in America now pushes toward the same ends.

Also strange is the fact that—unlike persons in, say, 1957—we now *know*, through compelling, irrefutable social science evidence that marriage is good for society, good for adults, and good for children. Books such as Glenn Stanton's *Why Marriage Matters* (1997), Linda J. Waite and Maggie Gallagher's *The Case for Marriage* (2000), and Bridget Maher's *A Family Portrait* (2002) show that traditional marriage is a great and irreplaceable social gift; *every good government* has a vital interest in encouraging as many traditional marriages as possible. Under their domain, adults are significantly—and often vastly—healthier, happier, safer, wealthier, and longer living. The children of intact traditional marriages are also much healthier in body, spirit, and mind, more successful in school and life, and much less likely to use illegal drugs and alcohol or run afoul of the justice system. These traditional marriages dramatically reduce public welfare costs, raise government revenues, and produce a more-engaged citizenry.[7] And yet, the very governments that benefit from intact traditional marriages often conspire to weaken them.

In this time of confusion, perhaps it is appropriate to ask the more fundamental question: *Just what is marriage?* The ancient Greeks had one answer. According to a legend passed on by Plato, there was once a being with both male and female natures who offended the gods and, as punishment, was divided into male and female halves. Even since, man and woman must find their missing half; when they do, they are rebound in marriage. The Book of Genesis, held sacred by Jews, Christians, and Muslims alike, has another answer: "So God created man in his own image, in the image of God he created him; male and female he created them. And God blessed them, and God said to them, 'Be fruitful and multiply and fill the earth'.... Therefore a man leaves his father and his mother and cleaves to his wife, and they become one flesh."[8] The nineteenth-century French writer Louis de Bonald, who helped to lay the foundations for modern social science, defined marriage as "a potential society," becoming "an actual society" only with the birth of the first child: "In a word, the reason for marriage is the production of children."[9] Compare these content-rich images to that of modern sociologists, who describe "the unique character" of marriage as being simply "public approval and recognition"; that is, something, anything, is "marriage" if the "public" says so.[10]

I now wish to offer my own rough definition of marriage and draw out certain policy implications, and will do so through five images.

First: Marriage is Peculiarly American

One popular view sees Americans, among the world's peoples, as specially or uniquely committed to individualism, personal autonomy, and the cultivation of the self. Some analysts argue that this attitude goes back even to the colonial days before the American Revolution.[11]

More careful history tells a very different story. As Colgate University political scientist Barry Alan Shain reports in his wonderfully revisionist book, *The Myth of American Individualism*:

> It appears that...most 18th-century Americans cannot be accurately characterized as predominately individualistic.... The vast majority of Americans lived voluntarily in morally demanding agricultural communities shaped by reformed-Protestant social and moral norms. These communities were defined by overlapping circles of family—and community—assisted self-regulation and even self-denial.[12]

Indeed, the evidence strongly suggests that America has long sustained an unusually strong culture of marriage. *Ben Franklin saw it*, attributing early and nearly universal marriage during the mid-eighteenth century to America's abundance of land and opportunity.

"Marriages in America are more general, and more generally early, than in Europe," he wrote, with both marriage and birth rates *twice as high* as found among the residents of Old Europe.[13] Twenty years later, *Adam Smith saw it*, attributing America's culture of marriage to a thriving economy:

> The most decisive mark of the prosperity of any country is the increase in its number of inhabitants…. The value of children is the greatest of all encouragements to marriage. We cannot, therefore, wonder that the people in America should generally marry very young.[14]

Alexis de Tocqueville saw it during his mid-nineteenth-century visit to America:

> There is certainly no country in the world where the tie of marriage is more respected than in America, or where conjugal happiness is more highly or worthily appreciated…. While the European endeavors to forget his domestic troubles by agitating society, the American derives from his own home that love of order which he afterwards carries with him into public affairs.[15]

American sociologists saw it in the middle of the twentieth century, when the *average* age for first marriage fell to twenty for women and twenty-two for men. By 1960, 90 percent of women aged twenty-five to twenty-nine and 80 percent of men of the same age range had already married. By age forty, 95 percent of all Americans were or had been married.[16]

How did this American culture of marriage work? Allow me here a personal story. My higher education began at a Lutheran liberal arts school along the Mississippi River in Illinois, Augustana College. When I arrived there in September 1967, as a freshly scrubbed first year student, the oft-told moral turmoil of the 1960s had not quite yet reached our campus. Instead, the college president greeted us new students and our parents in an assembly, where he noted jovially: "Look around you. You may be sitting next to your future husband or wife and your future in-laws." Everyone giggled or laughed, but he spoke the truth. The Augustana campus, like most colleges of the time, was the place where one expected to—and did— meet one's future husband or wife. I know I did, and so did most of my friends. The expectation of marriage was in the very air: marriage was assumed to be your next life step; all the cultural and institutional signals pointed that way.

Today, this assumption and the same signals are not found on most college and university campuses. A prominent exception is

Brigham Young University, now the nation's largest private university. There, the expectations of *early maturity and early marriage* still exist—in everything from the prevailing atmosphere of the school to the statuary on the campus grounds that features positive images of motherhood, fatherhood, children, and home.

Oddly, America's culture of marriage also survives in another, much-more-unexpected place: Hollywood. What do the following popular films have in common: *My Big Fat Greek Wedding*; *Maid in Manhattan*; *Sweet Home Alabama*; *Kate and Leopold*; *Notting Hill*; *Runaway Bride*; *You've Got Mail*; *Pretty Woman*; and *Sleepless in Seattle*? My daughters call them "chick flicks." A better label might be "marriage flicks," for all of them cast marriage as the great, satisfying, and truly fulfilling event in a woman's life. None of these films, let alone the whole genre, could have been made in cynical, libertine, post-marriage Western Europe. The Europeans do not believe in Cinderella anymore; Americans still do. These films are distinctly our own: signs of a still extant cultural yearning for marriage and home.

Second: Marriage is the Union of the Sexual and the Economic

This is not my original observation. Rather, this is the classic definition of marriage long used by cultural anthropologists to explicate this institution: namely, men and women cooperate economically in order to produce and rear children. According to the great twentieth-century anthropological surveys, marriage as such is found "in every known human society."[17] Paleo-anthropologist C. Owen Lovejoy, writing in *Science* magazine, musters the evidence showing that men and women are drawn together by a natural affinity for each other: an *innate* desire for a lasting pair-bond. Indeed, he sees this development of economic cooperation in permanent pair-bonds as *the* key step in human social evolution; that is, as the essential reason for *homo sapiens'* survival and success.[18] It is certainly true that for thousands of years and for hundreds of generations humankind organized most economic tasks around the family household. The growth, preservation, and preparation of food; the provision of shelter; the construction of clothing; the provision of education and medical care—all of these tasks, and hundreds more, took place in the home. Woman and man, wife and husband, specialized in their labor, to be sure, according to their relative strengths and skills. The work of both, though, was homebound and essential to family survival. Said another way, the human family has been conditioned to life in self-sufficient homesteads—on the small farm or in the village.

Some cast the industrial revolution of the last 150 years as by far "the greatest technological change that ever occurred in human society"[19] and as the material source of contemporary challenges to marriage. Industrialism tore apart the natural home economy. More precisely, this revolution shifted the place of work from the home to the factory or office; it displaced the generalized productive skills of *husbandry* and *wifery* with exaggerated specialization and commercially purchased goods. For a time, the "breadwinner/homemaker" model emerged as a substitute, resting on exaggerated distinctions between husband and wife and seeking to preserve the home as a shelter for children. But even this compromise broke down, under ideological attack and a growing demand for female labor by the offices and factories.

There is much truth in this analysis. However, some go on to argue that a new family form is now needed: an "egalitarian" family, without role specialization or home production of any sort, that would accommodate the industrial impulse. But it will not work. I agree with Kingsley Davis that such an "egalitarian family system"—as seen today most fully in Western Europe—cannot be sustained. High levels of divorce and cohabitation combined with low birth rates actually "raise doubts that societies with this egalitarian system will [even] survive."[20]

The necessary alternative is to find new ways of articulating and advancing marriage as an economic partnership. Between 1948 and 1969, for example, the U.S. government *did* treat marriage as a *true* partnership for purposes of taxation, allowing married couples to "split their income" like all other legal partnerships. One clear result was "the marriage boom" of that era: a phenomenon that ended only after the elimination of income splitting.[21] In addition, sophisticated calculations from Australia show that the traditional "home economy" has not disappeared at all. Even in advanced industrial societies such as the United States and Australia, the uncounted but real value of continuing home activities such as childcare, home carpentry, and food preparation is still *at least* as large as that of the official economy.[22] Moreover, a growing number of Americans are actively reversing the industrialization of activities that were once the family's—this is how we should see home schooling, for example, now embracing over two million American children. Stronger marriages built on the enhanced specialization of husband and wife is one result.[23]

Third: Marriage is a Balance of Burdens and Benefits

Here, a libertarian perspective offered by Valparaiso University Law Professor Richard Stith clarifies the issues at stake. He notes that liberals and conservatives alike should agree that state registries of friendships are a bad idea. Indeed, at present, most kinds of friendships are totally unregulated in the United States. Most states have even decriminalized non-marital sexual relations or no longer enforce prohibitions. This means that, for example, the participants in same-sex unions are as free as anyone else to form long-lasting sexual friendships—and to seal them with promises, vows, or binding contracts—all without governmental approval and registration.[24]

Stith emphasizes that only one category of heterosexual union faces government registry: those entering legal marriage. But this should not be seen as a liberty or right. Rather, it is primarily a burden. For the most part, marriage legislation limits, rather than increases, individual freedom. Marriage laws commonly mandate the sharing of earnings and debts, compel obligations of mutual support, and limit rights to terminate the relationship.[25]

Why do governments leave most friendships free and unregulated, but continue to register and burden heterosexual unions? Stith replies:

> Everyone knows the answer: Sexual relationships between women and men may generate children, beings at once highly vulnerable and essential for the future of every community…. Lasting marriage receives public approbation…because it helps to produce human beings able to practice ordered liberty.[26]

Heterosexual unions can create a child at any moment, so the public has a deep interest in their stabilization from the very beginning. In contrast, same-sex unions are "absolutely infertile"; a public interest in their stabilization would come only in those relatively rare cases of adoption by same-sex couples; and only at the time of adoption, not at the beginning of such a relationship. The relatively few benefits adhering to legal marriage (and not available through private contract)—such as social security provisions—are justified as compensation to those parents who make sacrifices—such as giving up a career—to raise children. "Such a parent voluntarily shares the vulnerability of his or her children by becoming a dependent," and deserves some minimal financial protection.

Stith asks other pertinent questions: Do we really want expanded government regulation of friendships? Gun owners, he notes, see ominous portents in all gun registration schemes. "How can gays and lesbians be sure registry lists won't be harmful in the end?" Why limit the extension of marriage registration and benefits just to unions based on a couple? Or just on sexual behavior? Since the potential generation of children is no longer the criteria, why shouldn't all close friendships be registered and granted benefits?[27]

Problematically, as qualification for the benefits adhering to marriage expands, so do the costs, which usually diminishes the net average value of the benefit. It is instructive here to note that the extension of "marriage rights" to same-sex couples in Sweden occurred parallel to the stripping from "marriage" of any meaningful legal status or economic benefit. The label was gained; but it carried no real advantage and came at the cost of ending protections for vulnerable children and self-sacrificing natural parents.

Fourth: Marriage is a Communal Event

It takes a poet to remind us here that marriage is more than a bond between two people. The Kentuckian Wendell Berry underscores that marriage also exists to bind the couple as "parents to children, families to the community, the community to nature." The new bride and groom "say their vows to the community as much as to one another, and the community gathers around them to hear and to wish them well, on their behalf and on its own." The very health and future of the community depends on the successful endurance of these vows. They bind the lovers to each other, "to forebears, to descendants...to Heaven and earth." Marriage is "the fundamental connection without which nothing holds."[28] Even the touch of one married lover to another

> ...feelingly
> persuades us what we are:
> one another's and *many others*...
> How strange to think of *children*
> *yet to come*, into whose making
> we will be made...[29]

Berry insists that sexual love, mediated through marriage, "is the heart of community life," the force connecting persons to the Creation and to the earth's abundance and fertility. Using a favorite metaphor, Berry says that marriage "brings us into the dance that holds the community together and joins it to its place."[30]

This community-building task of marriage underscores the special tragedy of the "no-fault divorce" revolution. Until the late 1960s, all American states required a finding of fault—such as adultery, cruelty, or desertion—before a divorce could occur. Designed to reduce acrimony in divorce, the introduction of "no-fault" provisions among the states over the last four decades actually saw acrimony merely shift to other issues, such as child custody.[31] Designed to reduce court time devoted to nasty family conflicts, "[t]he switch from fault divorce law to no-fault divorce law [actually] led to a measurable increase in the divorce rate."[32] Most importantly, the loss of the concept of fault in divorce cases meant abandoning the shared understanding that the breaking apart of a marriage was also a kind of crime against the community. Children, neighbors, friends, the local community itself would all be affected—almost always negatively—by the divorce decree. It is still important that someone be held accountable—"at fault"—for this unique kind of blow against community. But in this, we now fail.

Fifth and Finally: Marriage is Political

This is true in a narrow sense, such as the finding recently reported in *Business Week* that women are more likely to vote Democratic after a divorce and more likely to vote Republican after a marriage.[33]

But I am more interested in marriage as "political" in the broad sense, as explained by the English journalist G. K. Chesterton. He understands the family to be as a "triangle of truisms, of father, mother and child," an "ancient" institution that preexists the state and one that "cannot be destroyed; it can only destroy those civilizations which disregard it." This "small state founded on the sexes is at once the most voluntary and the most natural of all self-governing states." Modern governments seek to isolate individuals from their family, the better to govern them; to divide in order to weaken. But the family is self-renewing, an expression of human nature, which builds on the natural state of marriage. "The ideal for which [marriage] stands in the state is liberty," Chesterton writes. It stands for liberty because it is "at once necessary and voluntary. It is the only check on the state that is bound to renew itself as eternally as the state, and more naturally than the state." It creates "a province of liberty" where truth can find refuge from persecution and where the good citizen can survive the bad government.[34]

In sum, I see marriage as *specially American*, as *the union of the sexual and the economic*, as *a fruitful balance of burdens and benefits*, as *a communal event*, and as *political* in its essence. What policy implications would I draw from this analysis? Briefly:

- The states should reintroduce "fault" into their laws governing divorce. So-called "covenant marriage" measures, which create a voluntarily entered, higher-tiered marriage requiring a finding of fault for dissolution, are a relatively painless way to start the process. Ideally, fault would be reintroduced in divorce law across the board, in order to underscore the communal nature of marriage and the social gravity of divorce.

- All governments should treat marriage as a full economic partnership. At the federal level, this would mean reintroducing true "income splitting" in the federal income tax (which would also eliminate the most notorious "marriage penalty"). At the state level, this principle would encourage broader application of the "community property" concept inherited from the old Hispanic law codes of the American Southwest.

- The legal status of marriage, and any benefits that it confers, should be restricted to the monogamous bonds of women to men; simply and precisely because this is where children come from. The health and good order of our communities and nation depend on these strong marriages. Ideally, this ancient principle will continue to be recognized by the fifty states. If necessary, an amendment to the U.S. Constitution to protect marriage, as so defined, would be justified as a shield from harmful social engineering. In deference to the principle of liberty, other human friendships and relationships are properly left unregulated and unregistered.

- The renewal of an American culture of marriage will rely primarily on community and religious impulses. All the same, it is appropriate for federal and state public welfare programs (such as TANF grants) to seek ways to encourage and affirm marriage among aid recipients. These are not—and never have been—strictly private choices. The public interest is deeply involved in the state of marriage. The *welfare* of children and the *future* of this nation require the creation and maintenance of strong, married couple homes. The federal government can here play an affirmative role.

Notes

1. Data from *The Statistical Abstract of the United States*, 2002 and earlier editions. See also: Kingsley Davis, ed., *Contemporary Marriage: Comparative Perspectives on a Changing Institution* (New York: Russell Sage Foundation, 1985): 39.
2. From: "Talking About the Freedom to Marry," Lambda Legal, June 20, 2001, at: http://www.lambdalegal.org/cgi-bin/iowa/documents/record?record=47.
3. From: Robert Pear, "Legal Group Urges States to Update Their Family Law," *New York Times* (Nov. 30, 2002): 1-2.
4. Harry Willekens and Kirsten Scheive, "Introduction: The Deep Roots, Stirring Present, and Uncertain Future of Family Law," *Journal of Family Law* 28 (2003): 5-14.
5. By a Woman Resident of Russia, "The Russian Effort to Abolish Marriage," *The Atlantic Monthly* (July 1926): 4.
6. See: Allan Carlson, *The Swedish Experiment in Family Politics: The Myrdals and the Interwar Population Crisis* (New Brunswick, NJ: Transaction Books, 1990): chapter 7.
7. See: Glenn T. Stanton, *Why Marriage Matters: Reasons to Believe in Marriage in Postmodern Society* (Colorado Springs, CO: Pinon Press, 1997); Linda J. Waite and Maggie Gallagher, *The Case for Marriage: Why Married People are Happier, Healthier, and Better Off Financially* (New York: Doubleday, 2000); and Bridget Maher, ed., *A Family Portrait* (Washington, DC: Family Research Council, 2002).
8. Genesis 1: 27-28; 2:24. *Revised Standard Version*.
9. Louis de Bonald, *On Divorce*, trans. and ed. by Nicholas Davidson (New Brunswick, NJ: Transaction Publishers, 1992): 63-64.
10. Davis, *Contemporary Marriage*, p. 4.
11. See, for example: Bernard Bailyn, *Education in the Forming of American Society: Needs and Opportunities for Study* (Chapel Hill: University of North Carolina Press, 1960); and Jay Fliegelman, *Prodigals and Pilgrims: The American Revolution Against Patriarchal Authority, 1750-1800* (Cambridge, England: Cambridge University Press, 1982).
12. Barry Alan Shain, *The Myth of American Individualism: The Protestant Origins of American Political Thought* (Princeton, NJ: Princeton University Press, 1994): xvi.
13. Benjamin Franklin, "Observations Concerning the Increase of Mankind [1755]," in Leonard W. Labaree, ed., *The Papers of Benjamin Franklin*, Vol. 4 (Yale University Press, 1961): 228.
14. Adam Smith, *The Wealth of Nations* [1776]: Book 1, Chapter 8, "Of the Wages of Labour," at http://geolib.com/smith.adam/won1.-08.html.
15. Quoted at: http://www.nccs.net/newsletter/jan00nl.html, p. 2.
16. Davis, *Contemporary Marriage*, pp. 31-32.
17. George P. Murdoch, *Social Structure* (New York: The Free Press, 1965 [1949]).
18. C. Owen Lovejoy, "The Origin of Man," *Science* 211 (Jan. 23, 1981): 348.
19. Kingsley Davis, "Wives and Work: A Theory of the Sex-Role Revolution and Its Consequences," in Sanford M. Dornbusch and Myra H. Strober, eds., *Feminism, Children and the New Families* (New York: The Guilford Press, 1988): 71.
20. Davis, "Wives and Work," pp. 79-80, 82, 84.
21. See: Allan Carlson, "Taxing the Family: An American Version of Paradise Lost?" *Family Policy Review* 1 (Spring 2003): 1-20.
22. See: Duncan Ironmonger, "The Domestic Economy: $340 Billion of G.H.P.," in B. Muehlenberg, ed., *The Family: There is No Other Way* (Melbourne: Australian Family Association, 1996): 132-46.

23. See: Lawrence M. Rudner, "Scholastic Achievement and Demographic Character-
     istics of Home School Students in 1998," *Education Policy Analysis Archives* (Mar.
     23, 1999): 7-8, 12.
24. Richard Stith, "Keep Friendship Unregulated," *The Cresset* (Easter 2003): 47-49.
25. For a summary of these burdens, see: Michael S. Wald, "Same-Sex Couples:
     Marriage, Families, and Children: The Legal Consequences of Marriage,"
     Stanford University Law School (1999); at http://216.239.37.100/
     search?q=cache:6Vzgi3iFC7wJ:lawschool.stanford.edu/faculty/wald/co...
26. Stith, "Keep Friendship Unregulated," p. 47.
27. Ibid., pp. 47-48.
28. Wendell Berry, *Sex, Economy, Freedom and Community* (New York and San Fran-
     cisco: Pantheon Books, 1992, 1993): 120-21, 133, 139.
29. Wendell Berry, *A Timbered Choir: The Sabbath Poems, 1979-1997* (Washington,
     DC: Counterpoint, 1998): 99. Emphasis added.
30. Berry, *Sex, Economy, Freedom and Community*, p. 133.
31. See: Bryce Christensen, "No-Fault Divorce and the Family: The New Negative
     Sum Game," *The Family in America* 7 (Feb. 1993): 1-8.
32. Paul A. Nakonezny, Robert D. Shull, Joseph Lee Rodgers, "The Effect of No-Fault
     Divorce Law on the Divorce Rate Across the 50 States and Its Relation to Income,
     Education, and Religiosity," *Journal of Marriage and the Family* 57 (1995): 477-
     88.
33. Gene Koretz, "Divorce and Women Voters," Mar. 11, 2002; at: http://
     www.businessweek.com:/print/magazine/content/02_10/c3773041.htm?pi.
34. G. K. Chesterton, *Family, Society, Politics*, Vol. 4 of *The Collected Works of G.K.
     Chesterton* (San Francisco: Ignatius Press, 1987): 237, 242-45, 252-56.

2

Recrafting American Population Policy for a Depopulating World

Existing American population policy largely rests on two documents crafted thirty years ago, during the presidency of Richard Nixon.

On the domestic side, the 1972 Report of the President's Commission on Population Growth and the American Future provided the historic rationale for an aggressive federal campaign in *favor* of birth limitation and against the dreaded "third" American child. The Commission rejected the American "population growth ethic" that "more is better," concluding that "no substantial benefits would result from continued growth of the nation's population." The number of children "born now will seriously affect our lives in future decades," it said; indeed, the excessive number of American children could already be blamed for the country's so-called "crisis of spirit—environmental deterioration, racial antagonisms, the plight of the cities," and—amazingly—even the Vietnam War. A later passage darkly labeled the Baby Boom generation a "new wave of humanity," one that bore responsibility for virtually every national problem, from overcrowded schools to high traffic accident rates to general unease.

Astonishingly, the Commissioners admitted that, in 1971, the American fertility rate had in fact already fallen below the zero growth level for the first time in the nation's history: their goal had already been achieved. And yet, the Report still attacked the idea of a "birth death" or "baby bust" as phony. Instead, it mounted a full assault on the three-child family. The Commission warned that a three-child system would produce a population of 300 million by 1995 and a billion by 2070; a two-child per family system would slow growth to 325 million by 2070, saving the nation from a host of perils. One

15

particularly foolish map showed the lake regions of Illinois, Wisconsin, and Minnesota running out of water by 2020, due solely to this dreaded "three-child family" system.

While not directly assaulting religion, the Commission used the code words "tradition" or "custom" to make the same point, linking such "custom" to "ignorance" for good measure:

> Our immediate goal is to modernize demographic behavior in this country: to encourage the American people to make population choices, both in the individual family and society at large, on the basis of greater rationality rather than tradition or custom, ignorance or chance.

Commission recommendations included open propaganda in the schools in favor of population control, the promotion of "sex education" for all ("especially" in the schools), the distribution of "prophylactic information and services" to minors, and the legalization of abortion "along the lines of the New York State statute."[1]

On the foreign policy side, one of President Richard Nixon's last acts before resigning in disgrace was to direct the National Security Council to prepare a *secret* "study of the impact of world population growth on U.S. security and overseas interests." The result was National Security Study Memorandum (NSSM) #200, dated December 10, 1974.

The document focused on a United Nations' estimate of 3.6 billion persons in the world in 1970, with a median projection of 6 to 8 billion by the year 2000 and 12 billion by 2075. "Massive famines" were probable consequences, it said, as were slowed economic growth, severe resource shortages, and "high and increasing levels of child abandonment, juvenile delinquency, chronic and growing underemployment and unemployment, petty thievery, organized brigandry, food riots, separatist movements, communal massacres, revolutionary actions, and counter-revolutionary coups." Among the less developed countries, disruptive internal migrations, high numbers of young people, and "pressures for foreign migration" also could be predicted. These developments, the NSC staff concluded, "point toward Malthusian conditions for many regions of the world." Accordingly, the Report concluded that continued global population growth posed a grave security risk to the United States.

NSSM #200 also argued that "[w]e cannot wait for overall modernization and development to produce lower fertility rates naturally." An "all-out-effort to lower growth rates" was imperative. The Memorandum set a goal of keeping maximum global population at no more than 8 billion, by achieving "a replacement level of fertility (a two child family on the average), by about the year 2000." Specific strategies included undermining the traditional role of motherhood and "concentrating on the education and indoctrination of the rising generation of children regarding the desirability of smaller family size." The NSC document did give a nod to "the right of individuals and couples to determine freely and responsibly the number and spacing of their children." Yet the spirit of the report was closer to the "Alternate" view placed near the end of Section I, which pondered the possible need for "mandatory population control measures for the U.S. and/or for others."

Most controversially, the U.S. government secretly targeted thirteen nations whose growing populations reportedly posed a special threat to American interests: India, Bangladesh, Pakistan, Nigeria, Mexico, Indonesia, Brazil, the Philippines, Thailand, Egypt, Turkey, Ethiopia, and Colombia. Declaring a kind of covert demographic war on this "Key 13," the National Security Council urged that limited American resources be focused on reducing future human numbers in these lands. Interestingly, the document did warn that "[w]e must take care that our activities should not give the appearance to the LDC's [Less Developed Countries] of an industrialized country policy directed *against* the LDC's." This meant that American policies to cut human fertility overseas should also be "ones we can support within this country"; there needed to be a unity between *domestic* and *foreign* population policies.[2]

The "Depopulation Bomb"

It is true that the Presidential Commission on Population Growth was torn by dissent and that key recommendations faced stiff opposition among a minority of the Commissioners themselves and at the Nixon White House.[3] It is also true that NSSM #200 remained secret until 1989, lest its country specific strategy stir up emotions overseas. All the same, these two documents did provide the philosophical framework for a range of policy innovations during this era: from passage of the Title X domestic "family planning" program to the legalization of abortion (by Supreme Court fiat) in all fifty states to the mobilization of the U.S. Agency for International Development

and related bureaus in favor of birth limitation and population control. Opposition by social conservatives bore only limited fruit: U.S.
funds could not be used to pay for abortions, neither domestically
(the Hyde Amendment) nor in foreign lands. Otherwise, the Malthusian policy victory was fairly complete.

Indeed, in 2003, the architects of this policy revolution might look
back on their work with a grim pride. Fertility is tumbling around
the globe. In the year 2000, the United Nations' Population Division
predicted a global Total Fertility Rate (or TFR; an estimate of the
average number of births per woman over her lifetime) of 2.1 by the
year 2050; only two years later, in 2002, the group revised that number downward, to 1.85. This means that the world's population would
peak mid-century at 8 to 9 billion (not far from the NSC goal of 8
billion), and decline thereafter. In an article for *Nature* magazine,
Austria's Applied Systems Analysis bureau even predicts a *decline* in
the world's population of 500 million by century's end. Among specific countries, Brazil's TFR has fallen from 3.4 in 1990 to 2.0 today;
Iran's from 4.0 during the 1980s to 2.0 today; Mexico's from 7 births
per family in the 1970s, to 2.0 today; and the USA also hovers around
the 2.0 figure.[4] Has population stabilization built around the two-child
family system in fact been achieved? Has the environment been saved
from the catastrophe of excess number numbers?

Alas, the answers are "No." It turns out that there is no such thing
as population stability, except as an ephemeral and relatively brief
transition point. The very forces that have reduced average family
size from a natural level of seven children to two *also* appear to
press fertility reduction well below the *2.1* replacement figure, creating a different reality: *depopulation*. We may actually see the human future in Europe.

In 2003, the threat and reality of depopulation—once dismissed
as rightwing fantasies—have gone mainstream. The *New York Times*
highlighted this year "an increasingly worrisome reality for Italy and
other European countries whose fertility rates have plummeted over
the last decades, shifting one-child families close to the statistical
norm." Spain, Sweden, Germany, Russia, Greece, and Italy—to name
but a few—now face "the spectre of sharply winnowed and less
competitive work forces, surfeits of retirees, and pension systems
that will need to be cut back deeply." In some parts of Europe (such
as the Italian Province of Ferrara and German Saxony), fertility has

fallen to an average of .85 children born to women over their life-time, barely 40 percent of even the zero growth level. In northern Europe, marriage has been replaced by low-fertility cohabitating unions. In southern Europe, young men and women refuse to form unions of any kind.[5] Fertility decline has been particularly striking since 1990. By 2050, in consequence, most young Europeans will have neither brother nor sister, nor aunt nor uncle, nor cousins: so undoing even the extended family. "What we're seeing right now is a revolution in fertility," says Joseph Chamie, director of the United Nations Population Division. *The child is vanishing.*[6]

America's leading scientific and environmental journals also now convey a new reality. The March 28 edition of *Science* reports "Europe's Population at a Turning Point." It notes that the concept of *"population momentum* measures the effect of current age struc-ture on future population growth." In the year 2000, Europe's "mo-mentum" shifted from positive to "negative." If the European Union's current Total Fertility Rate of 1.5 remains unchanged through 2020, the EU will lose a quarter of its population—or 88 million persons—by century's end. The "dependency burden" of workers would nearly double, as well.[7]

But perhaps this will be good for the environment? Alas, this does not appear to be true. A recent article in the influential journal *Na-ture* reports a peculiar development: while Italy's population is in absolute *decline*, with *deaths* outnumbering births, the number of separate *households* is *growing*: a net increase of *6 million* in recent decades. Why? The answer is simple: *fewer marriages*, *more di-vorces*, and *fewer children* there have sharply reduced average house-hold size. In central Stockholm, Sweden, as another example, two-thirds of all households are lone individuals, who consume on a per capita basis much greater resources—from fuel to food—than do the vanishing large families. Counter-intuitively, it turns out that *the retreat from marriage* and *fertility decline* actually accelerate urban sprawl and environmental decay.[8]

Developed nations in Asia show the same turn toward depopula-tion. Japan has a TFR of 1.42, driven by a sharp rise in the number of adult women who are not married.[9] South Korea records a TFR of 1.5, down from 6.0 in 1960, and "a record for low fertility in a de-veloping country." The number of abortions there exceeds the num-ber of births.[10]

Flawed Explanations

Why the failure to achieve population stability? The answer, I believe, lies primarily in a flawed understanding of the cause of fertility change. The dominant explanation for most of the twentieth century might be labeled "materialist." Focused on economic incentives, it has exhibited "socialist" and "liberal" variations. Both show fertility decline to be the inevitable product of modern market economies. This assumption of inevitability has, in turn, given false direction to population policy.

The *socialist explanation* arose during the first Western birthrate crisis of the 1930s. The Swedish social democratic economist Gunnar Myrdal laid blame for fertility decline squarely on liberal capitalism. In societies under this system's sway, children became the chief cause of poverty. Given current social organization, the refusal of young people to bear children was natural, rational, and blameless, he said. The very persons who contributed the most to the nation's existence were dragged down into poverty, shoddy housing, poor nutrition, and limited cultural and recreational opportunities. Myrdal said that a voluntary choice between poverty with children or a substantially better living standard without them was what young couples now faced.[11]

Contemporary Social Democrats make the same case. As Peter McDonald explains, "[t]he risk-averse individual in a world that rewards market production is unwise to devote time or money to social reproduction [by which he means family creation]. Social reproduction involves altruism, that is, time and money devoted to others.... For the risk-averse in a free market economy, altruism is equivalent to foolhardiness." Specifically, the risk-adverse woman will be sure to be able to support herself and not to put herself in a position of dependency on a man. More broadly, the market is very short term in its orientation; indeed, financial markets punish individuals and firms for any short-term lapse. But childrearing is long term. Accordingly, rational persons choose to forego children.[12]

The "liberal" variation of the materialist theme is usually identified with Nobel Laureate Gary Becker of the University of Chicago.[13] Essentially, Becker and his followers—also called the "Chicago School"—argue that fertility decline is caused by shifts in the balance of economic costs and benefits produced by childbearing. They assume that all families in all times and places have some knowledge of contraceptive techniques, and turn to the rational control of births when it is in their economic interest. During pre-modern times, characterized by family-centered household production and high death rates, families behaved rationally by bearing many children. But a new development appeared during the nineteenth century, as fertility *fell* while per capita income rose. Becker attributes this new development to a rise in "the price of children." This so-called "price" depended, in part, "on the value of the time spent on child care by parents, typically mothers." The "foregone value" of time spent rearing children—which might have been sold instead on the emerging labor market—actually comprised over half of children's "shadow cost." Also, as infant mortality rates began to fall, parents shifted their reproductive strategy from "quantity" of children to "quality." In smaller families, they could invest more "human capital" in each child, and assume that it would survive. Becker emphasizes that the demographic transition toward low fertility was "not simply the result of 'modernization,' but itself help[ed] produce a modern economy partly by encouraging a greater investment in human capital."[14] The result was smaller families, but higher quality children and greater wealth.

Social Democrats have relied on their version of the materialist argument to justify a massive socialization of family functions and childcare costs as the way to encourage more births. Modern Malthusians have used the Chicago School explanation to argue that their project focused on birth limitation is in harmony with social evolution and economic growth.

Unfortunately, both portraits of economically rational parents making judicious fertility decisions soon ran into a problem: they failed to explain real historical changes. Charles Tilly reported that there was no historical evidence from Europe showing any relationship between declines in infant mortality and declines in fertility.[15] Detailed investigations of fertility patterns in Germany and England between 1550 and 1850 found *no* signs of fertility control guided by measures of poverty or changes in "the cost" of children. Rather, the areas studied all showed "natural fertility" throughout this period, where births to married couples reflected "the absence of deliberate birth control" and an average of six to nine children born into each family.[16] Moreover, recent massive demographic investigations for the European Fertility Project at Princeton University and The World Fertility Survey point to the incomplete nature of the materialist explanations. Until very recent times, these studies show, contraceptive use was confined to only a very few elites; and *marital* fertility in the West was "constant" at a high "natural" level, *despite* the fact that children often represented a *net economic loss* to their parents.[17]

"Ideas Have Consequences"

Australian demographer John C. Caldwell began to suspect that *ideas* and *values*, more than economic incentives, lay behind fertility decline. Even after the rise of industrial capitalism, Caldwell found that "the [traditional] family, hallowed by time and enthusiastically sanctioned by religion," could still prevail. What Caldwell called a "family morality" system could actually serve as a brake on the economic pressures toward social change; as he put it: "[t]his morality (and the [associated] high fertility) can long survive the growth of a substantial capitalist labor market, partly because it is supported by public religion and private adage." The Western world, he insists, had such a "family morality [system]…backed by the religion and outlook of the day" until about 1900, one that held the family economy and the market economy in balance. As Caldwell explained:

> The family system in the West depended on a sharp division of labour: the husband worked outside the home for wages or profits…while a wide range of [productive] activities (clothing, feeding, providing a clean and comfortable environment, child rearing) was undertaken by the wife with the help of the children (especially the daughters).

Resting on religious affirmation and a purposeful system of job and market wage preferences for fathers, this "two-tiered mode of production"—what we would call the bourgeois or Victorian home—sustained high fertility long after the materialist thesis said it should have disappeared.[18]

Caldwell concluded that the decline of this system had nothing to do with internal family economics. Again, "ideas" and "ideologies" were actually at play. Malthusian ideas gained hold of key elites among West European nations during the 1800s. These ideas eventually spread into the culture. A study of nineteenth-century English literature, for example, "showed that pride in large families declined well before there was any evidence of widespread fertility control." Birth limitation then spread, "domino fashion," to other European nations. The key triumph in every case, Caldwell argued, was the "rolling back of religion's grip on—indeed, concentration on—sexuality" and the consequent "ignoring of the religious view."

The same process occurred in the Third World, where colonial masters in India, Southeast Asia, and Africa transferred their Malthusian views to emerging colonial elites. Eugenic ideas played a role as well, pushed by American organizations such as The Population Council, the Hugh Moore Fund, and The Rockefeller and Ford Foundations. As Caldwell explained:

> The challenge to reduce high Third World fertility necessitated the development of a *morality* that made contraceptive practice in the West not merely expedient, but respectable and increasingly praiseworthy. Almost incredibly…the discussion of "condoms" changed in half a century from being regarded as lewd and obscene to demonstrating moral merit.[19]

Other new demographic evidence points as well toward *religion*— its strength or absence—as *the* major influence in determining fertility.[20] This view holds that an economic shift (such as the change from "family" to "factory" production) is merely an incentive for fertility decline; it is "neither sufficient nor necessary" to explain demographic change.[21] Instead, the influence of religion on the beliefs of persons regarding fertility serves in practice as *the critical, necessary*, and *sufficient* variable: *only change here can lead to fertility decline*. As Belgian demographer Ron Lesthaeghe summarizes, "secularization"—which he defines as "the decrease of adherence to organized forms of religion"—is both "the most powerful variable at the outset of the fertility decline" and "the one with the longest lasting effect or the highest degree of persistence."[22] Without secularization, the evidence shows, fertility decisions would remain "in the realm of the sacred," whatever the economic situation. This suggests that pre-1850 fertility in Europe was "natural" and high because most Europeans were active Christians; they refused to reduce their family size, *not* out of ignorance, nor because of potential household economic gains, but because of their obedience to Christian teaching.[23]

It was the French Revolution that released a "total attack" on this family morality system, advancing individualism, materialism, and radical egalitarianism to replace the Christian family system. A century later, Protestants broke ranks with over a thousand years of Christian consensus (including teachings of their own theological founders such as Martin Luther), and started to turn fertility control over to the individual's secular conscience. This left only the Roman Catholic Church to offer resistance in Europe to this aspect of secularization in the late nineteenth and twentieth centuries.

In sum, the weight of the evidence shows that the "first demographic transition" in Europe—marked by the abandonment of "natural fertility" levels of six to nine children per family in favor of a TFR slightly over 2—was primarily a *religious* event. Secular ideas of individualism, rational calculation of economic gain, and materialism won out because Christian obedience to the Genesis command "be fruitful and multiply" waned. Put another way, the compelling new evidence strongly suggests that sharp fertility decline was simply a sign of societal wide religious retreat.

The Diminished Child

What about the "second demographic transition," the label given by demographers to the turn toward below replacement fertility that set in, among developed nations, about thirty-five years ago? Does it, too, have a religious explanation?

The answer is "yes." Following the celebrated—if brief—Marriage Boom and Baby Boom era after World War II, fertility decline resumed in Western nations; the critical year was 1964. Fertility soon tumbled well below the zero growth level; a massive retreat from marriage commenced; and Western societies seemed to lose all sense of inherited familial order. Dutch demographer Dirk van de Kaa has described the phenomenon as involving four transformations:

1. A shift from *the golden age of marriage* to the dawn of the *age of cohabitation*, where marriage is increasingly discarded in favor of informal sexual and living arrangements;
2. A shift from the era of the *king-child with parents* to that of the *king-adult pair with one*—and usually only one—*child*;
3. A shift from *preventive contraception*, designed to benefit the favored early children, to *self-fulfilling contraception*, designed to please the parents; and
4. A shift from a *uniform family system* of a married couple with children to *pluralistic families and households*, including the rapid growth of single-parent families.[24]

How do demographers explain these changes? The Chicago School theorists emphasize the role of women's wages in this change, arguing that at "almost every age and birth order, higher net women's hourly earnings [compared to men's] reduce the likelihood of birth."

Equal Pay Laws adopted in the 1960s and early '70s, they suggest, disrupted systems where higher net wages for men encouraged fertility.[25] Researchers looking at Japan trace that nation's sharp fertility decline to the increase in the proportion of married women who were employed, from 13 percent in 1963 to 42 percent in 1991, a change labeled "the most rapid increase on record in economically advanced nations."[26]

But among other analysts, suspicion remains that "women's employment" may be more *symptom* or *consequence* of the *second demographic transition*, than *cause*. Michael Murphy suggests that the Chicago School simply cuts out the "middle level" explanations in order to link fertility decline to "remote determinants," without showing how these actually work.[27]

The very pervasiveness of this "second" transition points to better explanations. David Coleman notes that remaining pockets of high fertility in Europe—such as in the rural *urSwiss* regions of Switzerland—all disappeared after 1964. So did pockets of higher "Catholic fertility" still to be found in Spain and Portugal.[28] Van de Kaa reports that *97 percent* of twenty-one-year-old Danish women now report having had premarital sex, essentially marking the full collapse there of the old sexual ethic. Lesthaeghe and Meekers show that only 20 percent of all European Community citizens above age eighteen have a meaningful link to organized religion; among young adults, the figure is closer to 10 percent.[29] Ronald Inglehart cites the sharp decline in votes for identifiably religious political parties in Europe after 1963 as a sign of what he calls "the silent revolution" in European values.[30]

Coleman concludes that ideas and values "may be more important than had been thought" in explaining the *second* demographic transition.[31] Lesthaeghe is more blunt. Recent changes in family formation and marital fertility, he says, are nothing new. They merely continue the "long-term shift in the Western ideational system" *away* from the values affirmed by Christian teaching (specifically "responsibility, sacrifice, altruism, and sanctity of long-term commitments") and *toward* a militant "secular individualism" focused on the desires of the self.[32] Accordingly, *secularization* or the retreat from religion emerges again as the key variable in understanding population decline.

It is important to note that the values of the new secular order, despite the rhetoric, do not in fact center on "freedom" and "choice."

Rather, the evidence suggests that those are transitional arguments, masking a new and quite negative view of children. Belgian researchers point to signs that European youth "appear to be extending nonconformism with respect to abortion, divorce, etc., to parenthood as well," agreeing in large majorities with statements such as "children need only one parent" and "children are no longer needed for personal fulfillment." Even those who choose to parent now do so "to satisfy their private needs," rather than to meet religious, family, or communal obligations. The new "tolerance" of alternate lifestyles at times comes near to *excluding* parenthood even as an option.[33] Van de Kaa notes the paradox that it was the arrival of "perfect" contraception—in the mode of the birth control pill—in 1964-65 that, instead of bringing "wanted" children within marriage, produced couples who could live outside of marriage "without fear of unwanted pregnancy and forced marriage."[34] Historian Philippe Aries, author of the classic volume *Centuries of Childhood*, sees "a new epoch, one in which the child occupies a smaller place, to say the least." Between 1450 and 1900, he notes, the Europeans had expanded the place of the child in their civilization. Levels of care improved noticeably, and the period of childhood became something precious. Looking near the twentieth century's end at a civilization with almost universal premarital sex, ubiquitous contraception, legal abortion, and record-low fertility, Aries concludes: "In like manner, [the child's] role is changing today, before our very eyes. *It is [now] diminishing.*"[35]

Can the Europeans turn this situation around? It is highly unlikely. To begin with, as noted earlier, the "momentum" of demographic change in the European Union shifted to the negative side in the year 2000. The very age structure of the population now makes fertility decline even more likely than during the prior three decades, when it was already sharp and sustained.[36] Moreover, most European policymakers are simply *oblivious* to the driving role of faith and values in the changes they confront. They commonly embrace materialistic explanations of cause, welcome the disappearance of motherhood as a vocation, dismiss religion as a superstition of the past, and place all their hopes in the Swedish model. Specifically, they call for full gender equality, the priority of the work line over the family, and generous daycare, paid parental leave, child allowances, and other welfare benefits as their policy solutions. But there is no evidence that these measures positively affect completed family size. To the contrary, such reforms seem to lock post-family, anti-child values into place.[37]

American Exceptionalism

Europe is dying; so may be Japan, also done in by a broad rejection of children. However, unlike the late 1960s and 1970s, when America was leading the global retreat from marriage and children, something different is now happening here: Americans are breaking free from the Malthusian darkness. The United States is the *only developed nation* in the world that recorded an increase in its total fertility rate between 1981 and 2000: from 1.81 in the former year to 2.10 in 2000, an increase of 16 percent, just back to the replacement or zero growth level. This was not, as some suggest, a function of a rising number of births out-of-wedlock. Between 1995 and 2000, even marital fertility rose by 11 percent, the first sustained increase in that number since the mid-1950s. Nor was this a function of America's greater ethnic diversity. The increase in fertility among Americans of European descent actually climbed by 19 percent after 1981, to a total fertility rate of 2.065. As *The Economist* magazine recently summarized, "demographic forces are pulling America and Europe apart.... America's fertility rate is rising; Europe's is falling. America's immigration outstrips Europe's.... America's population will soon be getting younger. Europe's is aging." By 2050, *The Economist* calculates a U.S. population of about 500 million, compared to an *EU* in demographic freefall, with barely half as many people.[38]

The best explanation for America's greater fecundity is the higher degree of religious identification and behavior shown by Americans, when compared to Europeans. Forty-five percent of Americans, in the year 2000, reported attending religious services during the prior week; in Europe, under ten percent. And believers do tend to have more babies. For example, a study of differential fertility among "white fundamentalist Protestants" found a total fertility rate 13 percent above the American average. Among "fundamentalists" who attended church weekly, the figure was *27 percent higher*.[39] To choose another example, the fertility of American Latter-Day Saints, or Mormons, is about 70 percent above the American average.

Importantly, this American exceptionalism is actually not new. Back in 1755, the American polymath Benjamin Franklin had published an essay on "Observations concerning the Increase of Mankind, Peopling of Countries, &c." Europe, he saw even then, had little surplus land and was already filled with manufacturers. But in America, "Land being thus Plenty...and so cheap that a labouring Man, that understands Husbandry, can in a short Time save Money enough to purchase a Piece of new Land sufficient for a Plantation, whereon he may subsist a Family." Americans were "not afraid to marry" because they could look ahead and see that their children when grown up could be provided for as well. The true "Fathers of their Nation," Franklin added, would be "the Cause of the Generation of Multitudes, by the Encouragement they afford to Marriage."[40] In a later essay, Benjamin Franklin also mused that *religious belief* could influence the rate of population growth, and that here, too, the Americans were very different from Old Europe.[41]

And this population difference also bore consequences. One demographic historian, looking at the eighteenth century, notes:

> [A]s early as the 1730s, some Americans came to look upon the rapid growth of population...*as God's sign of approval for the virtuous lives of the colonists.* In view of the role that the idea of virtue played in producing a revolutionary ideology, this perspective on population increase seems of more than passing interest.[42]

Edward Wigglesworth, Professor of Divinity at Harvard, told his fellow Americans in 1775 that regardless of the results of the emerging American rebellion against the British, the astonishing growth in American numbers insured that the weight of power would shift to them by 1825. This confidence inspired by surging human numbers appears to have enabled Americans to risk open confrontation with England in 1775 over constitutional and economic questions.[43] Stated more directly: America's fecundity—its abundant fertility—actually made possible the American Revolution.

America's current place in the world may also be a consequence of American exceptionalism in population. Consider that in 1900, the great powers of the world numbered five: France, Germany, Russia, the United Kingdom, and a newcomer—the United States of America. The next hundred years saw these basic demographic changes:

Nation	1900 Population	2000 Population	Increase
France	39 million	59 million	52%
Germany	56 million	82 million	46%
Russia	138 million	144 million	4%
United Kingdom	42 million	59 million	42%
United States	76 million	281 million	270%

In the year 2000, there remained only one great power—the United States of America. Perhaps these figures are proof again that demography is, indeed, destiny.

Moreover, recent economic theory has shown the inadequacy of the Malthusian model, which equates population growth with diminished human well being. Economist Julian Simon acknowledges the obvious fact that "Additional people [such as babies] do indeed dilute capital and reduce the standard of living when they first arrive." But, from a longer perspective, the increase in the number of "knowledge creators" and the "creation of new technology in response to increased demand" produce very different results: "Additional people are then seen to have a positive effect in the long run." He concludes that moderate population growth is good, even necessary, for sustained economic growth.[44]

Toward a New Policy Framework

What does this mean for the twenty-first century? For reasons of social and cultural health, national security, and economic growth, it is time to re-craft American population policy for a new century and a new reality.

The most important steps are philosophical, in the realm of ideas. The current administration would do the nation a great service by repudiating NSSM #200 as well as the Report of the old Commission on Population Growth and the American Future. They should both be labeled as out-of-date, misleading, *irrelevant*. In their place, the current administration could articulate new principles on which a twenty-first-century American population policy might be built, in both the domestic and foreign spheres.

These principles might include:

- The United States of America holds the family to be the fundamental social unit, inscribed in human nature, and centered on the voluntary union of a man and a woman in a covenant of marriage for the pur-

poses of propagating and rearing children, sharing intimacy and resources, and conserving lineage and tradition.
- The United States of America recognizes that strong families commonly rest on religiously grounded morality systems, which deserve autonomy and respect as vital aspects of civil society.
- The United States of America views large families, created responsibly through marriage, as special gifts to their societies deserving affirmation and encouragement.
- The United States of America recognizes that human progress—social, cultural, and economic—depends on the renewal of the human population. Moderate population growth is in the nation's best interest.
- And the United States of America underscores that the demographic problem facing the twenty-first century is *depopulation*, not *overpopulation*.

How might these principles translate into domestic policy? On the positive side, they give coherence and affirmation to the Bush administration's current pro-family tax reforms: the increase in the child tax credit to $1,000 per child, and the reduction in the marriage penalty. These principles also reinforce the faith-based initiative project and the marriage assistance program now starting up at the Department of Health and Human Services.

These principles also point toward dismantling Title X of the Public Health Services Act. This "backbone of family planning services" in the United States[45] currently sustains over 4000 birth control clinics across the country, the largest number operated by The Planned Parenthood Federation of America. The origins of Title X bear up to little scrutiny. The measure was part hysterical overreaction to the so-called "population bomb." It was part tacit racism: as one White House aide from the era explained, birth control "has become more of a Negro issue than a Catholic one."[46] And it was part surrender to negative, immoral forces: as an influential 1969 magazine article argued, the best way to reduce American fertility was by promoting the "anti-natalist" behaviors already found "among...our *covert* and *deviant culture*, on the one hand, and our *elite* and *artistic* culture, on the other."[47] Designed to discourage fertility of all kinds, including *within* marriage, Title X also encourages sexual hedonism, subverts parental responsibility, and purposefully targets teenagers and minorities for conversion to an "antinatalist" culture. In short, it encourages the very attitudes and behaviors that create the "depopulation" problem. Title X is an embarrassing product of discredited ideas; it should go.[48]

Relative to foreign policy, these principles point toward a re-channeling of all American aid *away* from "family planning services" and *toward* "family building strategies." Instead of support for condom distribution and Malthusian clinics, American funds could be restricted to:

- *Abstinence education programs* (premised on "chastity" before marriage and "fidelity" within), which have been successful in nations such as Uganda;
- *Marriage promotion initiatives*, perhaps reflecting successful projects in America;
- *Maternal and child health projects*, designed to *save* lives and *safeguard* future marital childbearing, not *prevent* them;
- And *economic development projects* that respect family autonomy and initiative.

Would this represent what *Newsweek* calls, in a dark whisper, "the globalization of American family values"?[49] In one sense, *no*. The purpose would not be to impose exact American models on other nations. Rather, America would be recognizing, with respect, the "family morality systems" that exist in other lands and that have also been under attack in recent decades by Malthusian and anti-religious forces.

But in another sense, *yes*. These principles would realign America with those nations that still acknowledge and respect a transcendent God and a religiously grounded family system. The outlines of such an alignment have already been exhibited in recent United Nations sessions, where the United States has found itself closer in morality and spirit to many Third World nations than to the dying lands of the European Union and the Asian littoral.

The future lies with those nations that fear God and affirm Life and Family. The U.S. of A., I believe, should take a necessary place in that vanguard.

Notes

1. *Population and the American Future: The Report of The Commission on Population Growth and the American Future* (New York: New American Library, 1972): 1-3, 7, 14-21, 62-63, 125, 137, 156, 170, 178, 192.
2. See: "NSSM 200: Implications of Worldwide Population Growth for U.S. Security and Overseas Interests," National Security Council, Dec. 10, 1974 (at http://www.africa2000.com/SNDX/nssm200all.html): 3-12, 60-64; and *Population and The American Future*, p. 3.
3. On this, see: Donald T. Critchlow, *Intended Consequences: Birth Control, Abortion, and the Federal Government in Modern America* (New York: Oxford University Press, 1999): 161-73.

4.   "Global Baby Bust: Economic, Social Implications are Profound as Birthrates Drop in Almost Every Nation," *Wall Street Journal* (Jan. 24, 2003): B1-B2.

5.   See: Frank Bruni, "Persistent Drop in Fertility Reshapes Europe's Future," *New York Times* (Dec. 26, 2002): A1, A10.

6.   "Global Baby Bust," pp. B1, B4.

7.   Wolfgang Lutz, Brian C. O'Neill, and Sergei Scherbov, "Europe's Population at a Turning Point," *Science* 299 (March 28, 2003): 1991-92.

8.   Jianguo Liu, Gretchen C. Dally, Paul R. Ehrlich, and Gary W. Luck, "Effects of Household Dynamics on Resource Consumption and Biodiversity," *Nature* 421 (Jan. 30, 2003): 530-33.

9.   See: "Japan's Declining Fertility: '1.53 Shock,'" *Population Today* 20 (April 1992): 3.

10.   "South Korea's Low Fertility Raises European-Style Issues," *Population Today* 19 (Oct. 1991): 3.

11.   Alva and Gunnar Myrdal, *Kris I befolkningsfrågan* (Stockholm: Albert Bonniers förlag, 1935): 98, 170.

12.   See: Cristos Bagavos and Claude Martin, *Low Fertility, Families and Public Policies: Synthesis Report. Annual Seminar, Seville, Spain, 15-16 September 2000* (Vienna: Austrian Institute for Family Studies, 2001): 16-18.

13.   John Cleland and Christopher Wilson, "Demand Theories of the Fertility Transition: An Iconoclastic View," *Population Studies* 41 (1987): 5.

14.   Gary Becker, "Fertility and the Economy," *Journal of Population Economics* 5 (1992): 185-201. Also: Gary S. Becker, *A Treatise on the Family: Enlarged Edition* (Cambridge, MA: Harvard University Press, 1991); John Ermisch, "The Economic Environment for Family Formation," in David Coleman, ed., *Europe's Population in the 1990s* (Oxford: Oxford University Press, 1990): 144-162; and John Ermisch, *The Political Economy of Demographic Change* (London: Heinemann, 1983).

15.   Charles Tilly, "Review of *The Decline of Fertility in Europe*," *Population and Development Review* 12 (June 1986): 326.

16.   See: John Knodel, "Natural Fertility in Pre-industrial England, 1600-1799," *Population Studies* 38 (1984): 225-240.

17.   John Cleland and Christopher Wilson, "Demand Theories of the Fertility Transition: An Iconoclastic View," *Population Studies* 41 (1987): 5-30.

18.   John C. Caldwell, *Theory of Fertility Decline* (London and New York: Academic Press, 1982): 158-63, 168-72, 175-76, 302-05, 311, 324.

19.   From: John C. Caldwell, "The Global Fertility Transition: The Need for a Unifying Theory," *Population and Development Review* 23 (Dec. 1997): 803-12.

20.   Cleland and Wilson, "Demand Theories of the Fertility Transition: An Iconoclastic View," pp. 22-24.

21.   Ron Lesthaeghe and Christopher Wilson, "Modes of Production, Secularization, and the Pace of Fertility Decline in Western Europe, 1870-1930," in Ansley J. Coale and Susan Cotts Watkins, eds., *The Decline of Fertility in Europe: The Revised Proceedings of a Conference on the Princeton European Fertility Project* (Princeton, NJ: Princeton University Press, 1986): 290.

22.   Ron J. Lesthaeghe, *The Decline of Belgian Fertility, 1800-1970* (Princeton, NJ: Princeton University Press, 1977): 230.

23.   Lesthaeghe and Wilson, "Modes of Production, Secularization, and the Pace of the Fertility Decline in Western Europe, 1870-1930," p. 270.

24.   Dirk J. Van de Kaa, *Europe's Second Demographic Transition* (Washington, DC: Population Reference Bureau, 1987): 11.

25. John Ermisch, "Economic Influences on Birth Rates," *National Institute Economic Review* 126 (Nov. 1988): 77-78.

26. Naohiro Ogawa and Robert D. Rutherford, "The Resumption of Fertility Decline in Japan: 1973-92," *Population and Development Review* 19 (December 1993): 726-727.

27. Michael Murphy, "The Contraceptive Pill and Women's Employment as Factors in Fertility Change in Britain, 1963-1980: A Challenge to the Conventional View," *Population Studies* 47 (1993): 240.

28. Coleman, *Europe's Population in the 1990s*, pp. 45-47.

29. Ron Lesthaeghe and Dominique Meekers, "Value Changes and the Dimensions of Familism in the European Community," *European Journal of Population* 2 (1986): 259.

30. Ronald Inglehart, *The Silent Revolution: Changing Values and Political Styles Among Western Publics* (Princeton, NJ: Princeton University Press, 1977): 216.

31. Coleman, *Europe's Population in the 1990s*, p. 40.

32. Lesthaeghe, "A Century of Demographic and Cultural Change in Western Europe," p. 429.

33. Lesthaeghe and Meekers, "Value Changes and the Dimensions of Familism in the European Community," pp. 232, 248, 260.

34. Van de Kaa, *Europe's Second Demographic Transition*, p. 25.

35. Philippe Aries, "Two Successive Motivations for the Declining Birth Rate in the West," *Population and Development Review* 6 (Dec. 1980): pp. 649-50.

36. Lutz, O'Neill, and Sherbov, "Europe's Population at a Turning Point," p. 1992.

37. As example, see: Bagavos and Martin, "Low Fertility, Families, and Public Policies," particularly p. 15.

38. "Half a billion Americans?" *The Economist* (Aug. 22, 2002).

39. F. Althaus, "Differences in Fertility of Catholics and Protestants are Related to Timing and Prevalence of Marriage," *Family Planning Perspectives* 24 (Sept./Oct., 1992).

40. Benjamin Franklin, "Observations Concerning the Increase of Mankind," in Leonard W. Labaree, ed., *The Papers of Benjamin Franklin*, Vol. 4 (New Haven: Yale University Press, 1961): 225-34.

41. In: Labaree, *The Papers of Benjamin Franklin*, Vol. 9, pp. 59-100.

42. Robert V. Wells, *The Population of the British Colonies in America Before 1776: A Survey of Census Data* (Princeton, NJ: Princeton University Press, 1975): 285.

43. See also: Robert V. Wells, *Revolutions in Americans' Lives: A Demographic Perspective on the History of Americans, Their Families, and Their Society* (Westport, CT: Greenwood Press, 1982): 78; and Robert V. Wells, *Uncle Sam's Family: Issues in and Perspectives on American Demographic History* (Albany: State University of New York Press, 1985): 30-37.

44. Julian Simon, *Theory of Population and Economic Growth* (Oxford and New York: Basil Blackwell, Ltd., 1986): 3, 169.

45. Sarah S. Brown and Leon Eisenberg, eds., *The Best Intentions: Unintended Pregnancy and the Well-Being of Children and Families* (Washington: National Academy Press, 1995): 219.

46. Simone Marie Caron, "Race, Class, and Reproduction: The Evolution of Reproductive Policy in the United States, 1800-1989," Ph.D. dissertation, Clark University, 1989 (Ann Arbor: University Microfilms, 1989): 14, 23-24, 50.

47. Judith Blake, "Population Policy for America: Is the Government Being Misled?" *Science* (May 2, 1969): 522-29.

48. For a broader discussion of Title X, see Allan Carlson, "The Bipartisan Blunder of Title X," *Family Policy* 13 (Sept./Oct. 2000): 1-4, 7-8, 12-15.

49. "Bush Family Values: The New Christian Crusades," *Newsweek* (Dec. 1, 2002).

3

The Fractured Dream of Social Parenting

Ambitious human minds have dreamed over the millennia of ways for parents to shed the task of childcare, in favor of social parenting. An early and remarkably complete vision of a society built on collective childrearing appears in chapter 7 of Plato's great dialogue, *The Republic*.

"A great deal—no, everything—hinges on whether or not [procreation and childrearing] happens in the right way," a student notes at the outset of this famed passage. Another reports that "the most difficult period" in a child's upbringing is the time "between birth and schooling." From these apt assumptions, Socrates the teacher cuts to a seemingly unrelated matter, arguing for the equal treatment of women in matters of education, public service, and work. "[S]hould female guard-dogs share with the males the guarding and hunting," he asks? "Or should they stay indoors, incapacitated by their bearing and rearing of whelps, while the males work and do all the overseeing of the flocks?" He urges the students toward the first answer. Human women on average might be physically and mentally inferior to men, Socrates admits. But exceptional women are superior to many males, and some of these women will have inclinations—"natures"—toward tasks normally done by men. "Therefore...we have to educate them in the same way."

"Friends share," the philosopher adds, which means that "all the women are to be shared among all the men. And that the children are also to be shared, with no parent knowing which child is his, or the child knowing his parent." Accordingly, the "children of good parents" shall go to the *crèche*, the collective nursery, where nurses "who live in a separate section of the community" shall care for them. These caregivers, poorer and inferior, shall gather milk for the infants from the natural mothers. When these milk supplies fail, more inferior women—"wet nurses and nannies"—shall be brought in to handle the "sleepless nights and all the hard work." This will make childrearing "very easy for the wives of the guardians," the ruling class, for this "is only right and proper." Meanwhile, the children born of "worse parents and any handicapped children of good parents" shall be left to die "in some secret and secluded spot," lest they taint the social order.[1]

Some commentators argue that Plato was not seriously advocating a collectivist society: it was more of a playful warning, an early and subtle dystopia. Yet others see the powerful rationality of Plato's vision suggesting a mental exercise meant to be taken seriously.

Serious Ideologues

We can be more certain that Friedrich Engels, Karl Marx, and Lenin had clear purpose in their advocacy of social parenting. As the former two wrote in *The Communist Manifesto* (1848), "The Communist Revolution is the most radical rupture with traditional property relations; no wonder that its development also involves the most radical rupture with traditional ideas." In the 1884 work, *Origin of the Family, Private Property and the State*, Engels explained "that the first condition for the liberation of the wife is to bring the whole female sex back into public industry," which demanded in turn "the abolition of the monogamous family as the economic unit of society." The practical architect of the Communist utopia, Lenin, spelled out in 1919 the implications of this demand. Despite the liberating legislation already passed by the Russian Bolsheviks, "woman continues to be a domestic slave, because petty housework crushes, strangles, stultifies and degrades her, chains her to the kitchen and to the nursery, and wastes her labor on barbarously unproductive, petty, nerve-racking, stultifying and crushing drudgery." A "real emancipation of women, real communism," would come only after a mass struggle to crush "this petty domestic economy" and replace it with a "large-scale socialist economy." Lenin pointed to "public dining rooms, day nurseries, [and] kindergartens" as the means to emancipate women, and he complained that even the Bolshevik press did too little to praise collective childcare centers:

> It does not give them enough publicity, does not describe in detail what saving in human labor...what emancipation of women from domestic slavery and what an improvement in sanitary conditions can be achieved with *exemplary Communist labor* for the whole of society.[2]

A more subtle and distinctly American case for the same goal came from Lenin's contemporary, the feminist visionary Charlotte Perkins Gilman. In her utopian novel, *Herland* (1915), Gilman describes a community inhabited solely by women. Birth is by parthenogenesis: the babies leap from the heads (perhaps ninety years later she would have written "from the petri dishes") of their mothers. As with Plato, Gilman envisions a new kind of motherhood: *not* a baby in the mother's arms or "a little flock about her knees" but rather a motherliness "which dominated society, which influenced every art and industry, which absolutely protected all childhood, and gave to it the most perfect care and training." To secure this quality care, the mothers of babies willingly pass on their children so that they might be reared by the very best specialists in early childhood education. As a resident of Herland explains to the visitors: "child-rearing has come to be with us a culture so profoundly studied, practiced with such subtlety and skill, that the more we love our children the less we are willing to trust that process to unskilled hands—even our own." In Herland, the brightest and most skilled citizens compete for the privilege of being caregivers to the collected young. The natural mother willingly places her own child in a group nursery, for "there are others whom she knows to be wiser. She...honors their real superiority. For the child's sake, she is glad to have for it this highest care."[3]

Written in a different genre, Gilman's book *Women and Economics* built a non-Marxist case for the inevitability of collective childcare: not through revolution, but rather as the consequence of social evolution in an industrial market society. Gilman noted that, even by her day, the new industrial economy had already radically altered the home. Gone from urban households were the hundreds of productive tasks that had once defined the family economy: weaving; spinning; sewing; soap making; laundering; carpentry; vegetable gardening; and so on. After these changes, women's tasks in the home numbered only three: cooking; cleaning; and early childcare. There was absolutely no reason, she continued, why these functions could not also be industrialized. Home cleaning could be done by teams of specialists working swiftly and happily (perhaps to be called "the Merry Maids"). Meal preparation could take place in centralized industrial kitchens and families could collect their warm food in bags at special windows (perhaps to be called "fast food").

And childcare could be turned over to industrial methods, as well. "It is in the training of children for this [modern] stage of human life that the private home has ceased to be sufficient, or the isolated, primitive, dependent woman capable," Gilman wrote. Compared to the trained childcare giver, the typical young mother was clumsy and inefficient, her home "a tangled heap of industries, low in their ungraded condition, and lower still because they are wholly personal." Lingering insistence on maintaining "a privatized family" held back the evolution of "our human motherhood." As Gilman explained: "No mother knows more than her mother knows: no mother has ever learned her business; and our children pass under the well-meaning experiments of an endless succession of amateurs."

Fortunately, Gilman continued, social evolution was ready to solve the problem. "The lines of social relation today are mainly industrial," she wrote. "Our individual lives, our social peace and progress depend more upon our economic relations than upon any other." For modern women, "loyalty to our work" was displacing loyalty to home and family. To advance social evolution to the next level, women must now enter "the higher specialization of labor," where paid work could grow in a widening range "till it *approximates the divine spirit* that cares for all the world." The childcare center would be the vital center of this heaven-on-earth.[4]

Dystopian Warnings

Not every visionary, of course, saw collective childcare as an ennobling act. The portrait of the *dehumanization* implicit to non-family care—and its linkage to other forms of human engineering—was most vivid in Aldous Huxley's 1932 dystopia, *Brave New World*. The novelist begins by describing a tour in the distant future of The Central London Hatchery, where its Director reminds the citizens "that in those [old] days of gross viviparous reproduction, children were always brought up by their parents and not in State Conditioning Centers." It was the God of Industrialism, "Our Ford or Our Freud," who was "the first to reveal the appalling dangers of family life. The world was full of fathers—was therefore full of misery; full of mothers—therefore of every kind of perversion from sadism to chastity; full of brothers, sisters, uncles, aunts—full of madness and suicide." Only the industrial organization of reproduction and childrearing, the Director states, had liberated humankind from these terrors. Fetuses now grew in artificial wombs. In the nursery, "eighteen hundred bottles" simultaneously fed "eighteen hundred carefully labelled infants" with "their pint of pasteurized external secretion." Up in the nap room others "listened unconsciously to hypnopaedic lessons in hygiene and sociability, in class-consciousness and the toddler's love-life." Those a bit older were in the playroom, "amusing themselves with bricks and clay modelling, hunt-the-zipper, and erotic play."[5]

Among certain American Progressives, though, such prophetic warnings went unheeded. Inspired by "the Bolshevik success" in transforming Russia and agreeing with Gilman that social evolution or progress pointed toward the enhanced industrialization of life, they constructed their own ideology of social parenting. In his influential 1918 volume, *A Social History of the American Family*, the Progressive historian Arthur Calhoun underscored the imperative: "The new view is that the higher and more obligatory relation is to society rather than to the family. The family goes back to the age of savagery, while the state belongs to the age of civilization. The modern individual is a world citizen, served by the world, and home interests can no longer be supreme."[6]

This view also drew on the arguments of the Chicago School of sociology, crafted by Joseph Folsom, Ernest Burgess, and William Ogburn. They, too, looked to the relentless march of the industrial principle through social life, and chronicled the family's loss of function, as experts and specialists assumed ever more tasks. It was logical and historically necessary, they held, for the care of infants and small children to pass through the same process. The frail nature of the modern family required that "schools, nurseries or other agencies" enroll many more children in the future so as "to conserve childhood." Only "society" had the requisite expertise to develop properly "the personality of *its* children."[7] In the same era, social psychologist George Herbert Mead argued that "social roles" such as "father," "mother," and "competitive business men" were largely learned through play. Non-competitive, gender neutral playthings properly presented in the childcare center could produce a new democratic type of children, reared to be independent in their moral judgments while cooperative in their social activities.[8]

These theories transformed the crèche or childcare center in key professional circles from a limited service for troubled families into a desirable institution in each child's life. The findings of the 1930

White House Conference on Children captured well this new spirit: "If the grouping of little children for a few hours each day for educational activities and for habit training through nursery schools is found to be desirable in itself, then this service should be extended on behalf of children generally, regardless of the economic status of their family."

Experimental childcare centers appeared across the United States during the 1920s, many of them attached to universities. The Laura Spelman Rockefeller Memorial Fund provided crucial early funding for these "child development" innovators. Their importance was twofold. First, by applying the new doctrine of social parenting to real children, these experimental centers laid the foundation for future expansion. Second, they trained a new cadre of specialists and advocates who, some decades later, would successfully proselytize for collective childcare.[9]

A Personal Tale

This process and the revolution it entailed might best be understood through the story of one remarkably influential woman, Alva Myrdal. While a single human actor can rarely be the necessary and sufficient force in producing broad social change, she comes closer for her nation *and* America on this issue than perhaps any other. Her life story also illuminates certain deeper truths about the daycare debate.

Born 1902 in Sweden to parents deeply committed to socialism, feminism, and non-violent revolution, Alva Reimers grew to be a committed ideologue as well. At age twenty-two, she married the twenty-six-year-old economist Gunnar Myrdal and they quickly emerged as leaders among Sweden's young socialist intelligentsia. In 1929, the Laura Spelman Rockefeller Foundation awarded both of them fellowships to study and travel in the United States during the 1929/30 academic year. Before leaving for America, they spent several months in England, where Alva dove into the study of educational theory. She reported to a professor back in Stockholm of her growing enthusiasm for the progressive concept of "the school as a substitute for the family."[10] Once in the United States, the Rockefeller Foundation directed her toward study of the "socialization of the child" and emerging theories of child psychology and pre-school care. She conducted research at the Child Development

Institute of Columbia University, the Institute of Human Relations at Yale, and the Child Welfare Institute of the University of Minnesota, all of which also enjoyed the Foundation's support. She made extended working visits to the Rockefeller Foundation's experimental pre-schools in Toronto, Winnetka (Illinois), and Washington, DC. At the University of Chicago, she worked with W. I. Thomas, Dorothy Thomas, and William Ogburn, who impressed on her their views about the functionless modern family and the need to build new collective structures for childrearing.[11] By the time for her return to Europe, Alva Myrdal had gained from these progressive American sources a passionate commitment to group childcare as historically ordained, socially necessary, *and* good for children.

She soon moved into political action. In 1931, she organized Sweden's first "study circle" for parents, where she underscored "the modern era's need for collective [child] activity" and the necessary construction of "a new parenthood" as part of "the evolution toward rationalization of human life."[12] The next year, she generated a huge public furor by announcing plans for building a high-rise "collective home" for Swedish families. The old family structure resting on the mother-at-home was failing, Alva Myrdal said. Urban industrial life had destroyed the household as a producing and consuming unit. Meanwhile, "paid work, productive work, is now a woman's demand, and as such a social fact, which lies completely in line with general tendencies of development." Birth control was also "a social fact" that had to be taken into account in planning for the future. Both the old "single family home" and existing urban apartments were totally unsuited to these new realities.[13]

Instead, young families should live in collective homes. Her high-rise designed by the famed modernist architect Sven Markelius would feature large central corridors linking family units. The latter would have a closet, a bathroom, cupboards, and bedrooms for the adults and older children. All meals would be prepared in a central kitchen and delivered to family units via dumb waiter or served in a central dining hall. There would be a collective lounge, library, sunroom, gym, and phone center. At the heart of the project, though, would be the collective nursery. The infant's section would care for children twenty-four hours a day, employing "highly trained attendants" operating in "the most hygienic conditions." The toddler section would care for children under school age, featuring "a well-lighted playroom," pedagogically correct playthings, and more "highly trained personnel."

Summarizing her purpose, Alva Myrdal called the existing Swedish "miniature family" an "abnormal situation for a child," one "almost pathological." The daily collectivized activity of small children in the daycare center was necessary so that they would be raised to be "effective members of modern society, not overexcited homebodies."[14] Where Gilman had never moved beyond dreams, Alva Myrdal actually saw her "collective home" through to completion in early 1936.

Yet her broader project had already moved far beyond a mere experimental building. In late 1934, she and her husband published a joint book, *Kris i befolkningsfrågan* ("Crisis in the Population Question"). Within a matter of weeks it had sparked Sweden's "greatest public debate" on social policy. The volume focused on the nation's birth rate, which in the early 1930s had fallen to the lowest level in the world. Depopulation and national ruin loomed, the Myrdals argued, as fewer Swedes married and fewer still had more than one or two children. Unlike conservative commentators, though, the Myrdals refused to condemn young adults as irresponsible, irreligious, and immoral. Rather, they said that Sweden's current social, economic, and political conditions had been so badly disfigured by liberal capitalism that the latter was actually responsible for the paucity of births. Children, economic assets in an agrarian world, had become liabilities under an urban, capitalist order; politicians took no account of the burden that children now formed. Young adults could defend their standard of living only by delaying marriage and reducing their fertility.

Building a New Order

The situation would not improve under the existing system, the Myrdals insisted. Only the radical reconstruction of the whole of Swedish life could restore fertility to a replacement level. This meant the implementation of central economic planning to guide future economic growth in more family friendly ways. It meant sweeping tax reform to shift the fiscal burden onto the unmarried and childless. It meant construction of a massive welfare state that would provide interest-free marriage loans to young adults, free education for the children, free school meals, state allowances for the purchase of children's clothing, subsidized family housing, free summer camps, and free family medical and dental care. It meant repeal of the laws banning the sale of contraceptives and a liberalization of abortion policy so that *all* parenthood would be voluntary and *all* children wanted. And, at Alva's insistence, it meant that women must be empowered to combine careers and motherhood; this required, in turn, a national commitment to state-funded daycare as normative and as a right.[15]

The book turned Swedish politics upside down. The Myrdals' approach stole pro-family arguments from the conservative parties, and turned "save the family" and "save the nation" into Social Democratic Party slogans. In 1935, the Socialist government created a Royal Commission on Population, to which Gunnar Myrdal was named; he soon emerged as its leading member and oversaw the preparation of a dozen major reports, all of which followed "the Myrdal line." The same year, the government also created The Investigative Committee on Women's Work; Alva Myrdal became its secretary, or chief of staff. The Committee had actually been formed at the urging of parliamentarians—Conservatives and Socialists alike—who complained about the "double wage" earned by families with working wives. But Alva Myrdal quickly turned the ideological tables. The Committee's principal report rejected all efforts to discourage women's employment. Instead, it held that society, economy, and government needed to be reorganized so that women could combine marriage and motherhood with paid labor. Maternity leaves with job guarantees, more part-time and temporary work, special arrangements for married couples to work close to each other, and expanded opportunities and subsidies for daycare were the policy imperatives.[16]

Also in 1935, Alva Myrdal published another controversial book, *Stadsbarn* ("City Children"), where she declared that, "small children do not belong in the city! At least not as cities are now constituted." Her answer, of course, was a national commitment to *storbarnkammare*, or daycare centers, which would free mothers to find suitable employment and give children the play, health, and educational opportunities not available to small urban families. Properly built and operated, she said, daycare centers were not a dangerous source of disease, as their critics changed. To the contrary, these centers opened opportunities for the improved expert monitoring of children's health. More importantly, Myrdal argued, they provided the means for socializing children in ways more appropriate to twentieth-century society. Playthings that were interchangeable between boys and girls would help end the "exaggerated" gender differences found in "troubled" middle-class homes, while collective group activities by small children would condition them for life in a cooperative socialist order.[17]

The next year, she created the Social-Pedagogical Institute in Stockholm, and became its first director. Funded by the housing cooperative, HSB, the Institute trained Sweden's first generation of daycare workers and kindergarten teachers. Through its work, Alva Myrdal redirected the goals and content of Swedish pre-school education to be in line with progressive American methods.[18]

Maternalist Reaction

But the Swedish juggernaut toward collective childcare, so carefully nurtured by Alva Myrdal, slowed over the next several years, and then reversed. The expansion of Nazi Germany in the late 1930s diverted funds, even in neutral Sweden, away from social welfare benefits toward defense. More critically, though, another vision of family life began to reassert itself within Social Democratic Party ranks. Called *maternalism*, it held—in one analyst's words—that "women were to be liberated *from* the labor market rather than liberated to participate in it." With deep roots in the labor unions, this attitude saw Alva Myrdal's egalitarian feminism as part of the problem, not the solution. Capitalists should not be allowed to claim the mothers, wives, and daughters of the working class, the argument went. Instead, true socialism meant enabling a man to maintain a wife at home giving her full-time care to the children. Under this strategy, the labor movement's goal should be to gain a "family wage" from employers for each male worker.[19]

As the pathos of war and national danger grew, this left-wing maternalism drove out Alva Myrdal's more radical formulation. The labor unions (collectively organized as the LO) negotiated in 1938 the historical *Saltsjöbaden* agreement, which crystallized job segregation by gender, reserving the better industrial jobs and the higher wages for their male members. The LO became Sweden's greatest champion of the family wage and it locked into place a "male breadwinner ideology." When a Second Royal Population Commission went to work in 1944, it rejected most of the Myrdal plan, including expanded daycare. Instead, it proposed creation of state *child allow-*

ances designed in part to help young mothers stay at home with their children. These went into effect in 1948.[20]

For a time, Alva Myrdal and her case for social parenting retreated from Sweden's political life. She came to the United States for five years, where she wrote and published *Nation and Family* (1941), an English language version of *Kris i befolkningsfrågan*, albeit stripped of more overt socialist and feminist language. Next, she took the post of deputy assistant secretary general for The Social Commission at the new United Nations. She was the highest ranking woman there; "third from the top," she liked to say. Her portfolio included women's, children's, and population issues, and she planted her ideology of a diminished family and a collectivized "new" childhood in international soil.

Meanwhile, Sweden settled into a remarkable period of traditional domesticity, encouraged by the maternalist worldview. Feminist analysts now call the 1945-67 period "the era of the Swedish housewife."[21] Policy encouraged the full-time care of small children at home. True, there was a rise during this period in the number of working mothers; but most of them had only school age children and most worked part time. Fertility climbed again; some talked of a Swedish baby boom. As late as 1965, only *three percent* of all Swedish preschool children were in some form of public daycare; and even half of these were in family daycare in private homes.[22] Moreover, there were few signs, visible or otherwise, of unhappiness among young Swedish women. By and large, they were content with their work in their homes as wives and mothers.[23]

But Alva Myrdal gained a second chance in the late 1960s. Radical change was in the wind throughout Europe: "Eurocommunism" on the march; Paris torn by New Left riots in 1967-68; Red Brigades terrorizing Italy and West Germany; and traditional Christian values—"responsibility, sacrifice, altruism and the sanctity of long-term commitments"—rapidly giving way across the continent to a militant "secular individualism" focused on the desires of the self.[24] Sweden, too, entered into what one leading historian calls "The Red Years," 1967 to 1976. At their core was a massive "gender turn" that would "radicalize" Swedish society.[25]

Alva Myrdal was again the key agent of change. In the late 1960s, she chaired an important Commission on "Equality" for the Social Democratic Party and LO that concluded, "there are strong reasons for making the two-income family the standard in the planning of long-term changes in social insurance."[26] No adult should be dependent on another, the report said. Marriage should be stripped of all legal preferences. Policies that favored the mother-at-home, such as the "family wage" ideal and the progressive income taxation of households rather than individuals, must also be scrapped. Special priority, her report said, should be given to expanding state subsidies for childcare. This would grant "equality" to women in the workplace and, at the same time, condition the minds of small children for a more egalitarian world.

"Red Sweden"

In 1972 a new prime minister came to power, the American-educated Olof Palme (a graduate of Kenyon College). Alva Myrdal joined his cabinet as minister of disarmament and Church affairs (despite being an atheist she controlled the appointment of bishops to the Swedish State Church). Fully under her sway, Palme addressed the women of the Party that year, declaring an end to the maternalist order. "In this society," he said, "it is only natural for both parents to work. In this society it is evident that man and woman should take the same responsibility for the care of the home and the children." Importantly, he added that "[i]n this society...the care of these future generations is just as naturally the responsibility of us all."[27]

The true revolution began. The Party abolished its Women's League, long the bastion of the homemakers. Women would now be "real members" of the Party, dealing with "common issues" alone. New policies made employment nearly mandatory for all women in their twenties and thirties. Surviving homemakers would pay dearly through crushing marginal taxes on their husbands. Small children moved massively into now heavily subsidized daycare: 460,400 held places in 1995, compared to only 23,400 three decades earlier.[28]

Yvonne Hirdman powerfully and correctly gauges the sweep of change here. She notes that women's work in this new Swedish order took on a peculiar quality. In the fields of agriculture and forestry, the number of working women actually declined, while in private industry it grew only modestly. However, in the service sector (heavily *governmental* in nature), their number rose from 269,000 in 1950 to 819,000 by 1990; in the education and health care sectors (exclusively governmental), the number of working women rose nearly *three* fold, from 282,000 in 1950 to slightly over 1 million by 1990. In short, "family politics" had been used as a lever to achieve something "truly revolutionary": the shriveling of private life and a massive expansion of the state sector as a means of securing "economic democracy." Pointing specifically to the experience of Alva Myrdal, Hirdman adds triumphantly:

> New ideas of gender replaced old-fashioned ideas about the couple. We witness [here] *the birth of the androgynous individual* (and I speak about the explicit ideal) and *the death of the provider and his housewife*. We thus witness old ideas popping up, ideas that had been buried for decades—but ideas that very quickly found their advocates and became developed: people, men and women, eager to *speak the new tongue of gender*.[29]

This is what the childcare debate is actually about. The core issue is not over choice, nor is it about the welfare of children, nor the needs of families, nor the natural course of social evolution in an industrial age. From Plato in the fourth century B.C. to the heirs of Alva Myrdal in the twenty-first century A.D., the core issue is a conflict of worldviews, of ideologies. On one side is a family-centric worldview that accepts the innate roles of men as fathers and women as mothers and that builds a social, economic, political order that will best nurture children. On the other side is a quest for an abstract and androgynous equality, one that willingly uses political power to crush the "natural difference" of men and women and the "natural institution" of the family home; and one that openly turns children into objects of experimentation, even exploitation.

The American Story

But perhaps Sweden is some odd exception? Perhaps the American story over the last seventy years is fundamentally different? In fact, it is remarkably the same; except that, just as Alva Myrdal's *Nation and Family* was a more cautious book than its Swedish predecessor, with *ideological* machinations cloaked by social science jargon, so too the advance of the daycare agenda in America has been ably masked by a politically-charged sociology. It claims objectivity, but actually serves the egalitarian agenda. Since 1970, ironically, "the Swedish model" has been repeatedly held up by American advocates as the new social ideal, complete with daycare as a right. And so, ideas born in progressive American institutions early in the twentieth century returned to America as "The Swedish Way" at century's end.

The details of the American story have been told elsewhere.[30] The broad contours, though, are clear and familiar. American "maternalists" active in the Democratic Party gained control of the Federal Women's and Children's bureaus during the 1930s and took prominent places in shaping the New Deal. They repudiated the experimental childcare work of the Rockefeller Foundation. Fiercely opposed to daycare, they sought a "family wage" for fathers, social insurance (such as widow's and homemakers pensions) for mothers, and fulltime maternal care for children. Even during World War II, they labored successfully to hold most mothers of young children in their homes and to keep new federal daycare centers for the children of defense workers limited and temporary (all centers would be torn down after the war). The American "marriage boom" and "baby boom" of the 1945-65 era were, in many respects, their legacy.[31]

In late 1968, though, equity feminist ideologues won control of the Equal Employment Opportunity Commission (was it a coincidence that a new American edition of Alva Myrdal's *Nation and Family* also appeared in 1968?). They used federal power to destroy the American version of the "family wage" and to elevate daycare into a civil rights issue. The 1970s were devoted to building the American daycare regime. In 1973, the United States actually came within a hair's breadth of creating a massive federal "child development" entitlement that would probably have surpassed even that of "Red" Sweden. Approved by a Democratic Congress over the objections of scattered conservatives (Senator James Buckley of New York warned that the bill would make the federal government the "arbiter of child-rearing practices in the United States...producing a race of docile automatons"), President Richard Nixon vetoed the measure. It "would commit the vast moral authority of the federal government to the side of communal approaches to childrearing as against the family-centered approach," he said. (Presidential aide Patrick J. Buchanan reportedly drafted the veto message.) The Senate sustained Nixon's act. This meant that American daycare advocates would have to rely instead on means-tested daycare grants for small children on welfare and generous universal tax credits for wealthier families and corporations that used or provided social parenting. But in practice, these almost proved sufficient.

Even the most radical consequence reported by Hirdman for Sweden has had its American parallel. The large majority of jobs that

American women moved into after 1965 fell into but a few categories: government employment; public education; welfare services; health care; and childcare. Tasks that had been done before by families in their own homes—primary health care, infant, toddler, and after-school care, maternal nursing, and so on—were turned over instead to the state. American women now worked for government rather than for their own families: "public patriarchy" some feminist theorists labeled it. Higher taxes, which fell with particular force on remaining one-income "breadwinner/homemaker" homes with three or more children, paid the cost.[32] Achieved incrementally and with few open ideological clashes, it might be called The Swedish model via The American Plan.

Internal Contradictions

It is true that the "maternalist" form of social organization had its own internal contradictions, which left it vulnerable to criticism. Most notably, American policy architects could never quite decide what to do with never-married mothers. As Jane Lewis has phrased it: "In the absence of a breadwinner, is the mother to be treated primarily as a mother or a breadwinner?"[33] Under the regime of Aid to Families with Dependent Children, they were treated as mothers, but this quickly became an incentive for more out-of-wedlock births and long-term welfare dependency. After "welfare reform" in the 1990s, single mothers were treated primarily as "breadwinners" and forced into the labor market. But this took an already incomplete family and broke it apart still further. State daycare providers were the primary beneficiaries.

However, the regime of social parenting bears its own contradictions, which—being more universal—can also be judged more serious. To begin with, there is mounting evidence that, contra Charlotte Perkins Gilman, childcare may be the *one* human activity that cannot be industrialized. The psychological evidence is overwhelming, and still mounting, that children in extended daycare—even very good daycare—are on average more aggressive, less sociable, and less emotionally secure—traits that, ironically, undo the key socialist goal of enhanced human cooperation. A few years ago, psychologist Stanley Greenspan of George Washington University summarized the six forms of true socialization that every child needs for its intelligence to develop properly: (1) an on-going, loving, intimate relationship with one—or at most two—caregivers; (2) uniquely tailored sights, sounds, touches, and sensations; (3) an "emotional dialogue" between adult and baby resting on long sequences of cuddles, sounds, and facial expressions; (4) long non-verbal dialogues using gestures to solve problems; (5) a creative dialogue through shared play; and (6) conversations using logic and reasoning. Three of the six, Greenspan reports, are impossible to achieve even in the best modern daycare centers.[34]

Second, social parenting is in the end dehumanizing. Since the emergence of Neolithic man until the end of the twentieth century—and despite the utopian dreams—every successful human community in every corner of the globe rested on the family as the cell of society.[35] Contra Gilman again, the key step in human social evolution had proved to be the emergence hundreds of generations earlier of the permanent sexual bond of man and woman, in order to protect infant life.[36] The Communists in Russia were the first to experiment with society-wide collective childrearing. The resulting social and economic disaster brought on by this perverse attempt at social engineering showed the dangers and costs of manipulating human nature. Characteristically, the feminist advocates of social parenting still talk about "defamilization" as their core project, one including "the right *not* to care" for others.[37] With Huxley's "Central Hatchery" not far away, we might safely conclude that feminist theory has reached its fated end.

Third, contra Alva Myrdal, the risks posed to infant and child health by daycare are not going away. True, massive regimens of antibiotics for all the children involved make the short-term situation often tolerable. But children in daycare are still at nearly 100 percent greater risk for contracting life-threatening diseases such as hemophilus influenza and meningitis. They are four and a half times more likely than home-cared children to contract infections and nearly three times as likely to need hospitalization. Daycare children are significantly more at risk of contracting upper respiratory tract infections, gastrointestinal disorders, ear infections, salmonella, herpes simplex, rubella, hepatitis A and B, scabies, dwarf tapeworm, pinworms, and diarrhea. And antibiotics are a fading asset: virulent new strains of disease resistant to these drugs now find their way into the centers.[38]

Fourth, daycare proves in practice to rest on class exploitation. As Plato honestly foresaw, a large part of the modern American childcare regime involves wealthy two-income families using tax subsidies to place their children in childcare centers staffed by low-wage female workers. Daycare employees are *not* the "superior" women dreamed of by Charlotte Perkins Gilman in *Herland*. One looks in vain for daycare workers profiled in *Town & Country*, or even *Business Week*. Rather, like eighteenth-century French wet nurses and nineteenth-century English nannies, twenty-first-century American childcare workers are commonly the poorest of the poor, distorting their own lives to serve their "betters."

Finally, also contra Alva Myrdal, social parenting built into the welfare state has not solved Sweden's—or Europe's—population problem. For a brief time in the early 1990s, some demographers argued that Sweden had found a way out of the again-looming disaster of depopulation. After falling to new lows during the radical 1970s, Swedish fertility seemed to be rising after 1983, and by 1990 had apparently reached a level just shy of the "replacement" level. An aggressive program of public daycare and paid parental leave seemed to have "reconciled" work and family. Perhaps this indicated "what lies ahead for other populations," suggested one analyst hopefully.[39]

Yet, it all proved to be illusion. Policy manipulations and new state money had only managed to affect the timing of births; completed family size changed not at all. Recalculations showed Swedens total fertility rate actually to be 1.6 (lifetime average births per woman), about 25 percent *below* the zero-growth level.

In fact, the now dominant Swedish values of "individualism and pluralism" threaten to overwhelm the ideal of intergenerational solidarity on which the Swedish welfare state itself had been built.[40] Relative to fertility, it turns out that the provision of essentially "free" daycare to working mothers is counterproductive, for the clear economic reason that it means the hiring of ever more women to provide the care, which raises in turn the aggregate social "cost" of children and so reduces overall fertility.[41] Indeed, demographer Heather Joshi points to the inherent futility of the Myrdal scheme by noting that so-called "women-friendly policies" such as daycare are now advanced in Europe to *increase* fertility while the *very same policies* are advanced (with *far more* success) in the Third World to *decrease* fertility.[42]

Matters have not gone quite so far in America. Despite the scorn they draw from American policymakers, many American parents still make the sacrifices needed to care for their own children at home. *Thirty* percent of families with three- to five-year-old children and making between $20,000 and $30,000 still give their children fulltime care. (Reflecting the "class" nature of modern daycare, only 13 percent of households earning over $75,000 provide their children fulltime parental care.)[43] Among families with younger children, the figure is higher still. Opinion surveys repeatedly show that the large majority of young parents want to provide their children with fulltime care; economic pressures and the clear federal preference for social parenting get in the way. According to a CBS News Poll, a full 74 percent of Americans endorse the idea of extending the existing "dependent care tax credit," now available only to parents using purchased daycare, to young families caring for their children at home.[44]

These facts testify to the resilience of Americans in the face of social engineering, and to the love of family and children as a defining quality of the American spirit. It is past time for American policymakers to reverse their puzzling course and to give young families real affirmation and real choices.

Notes

1. Plato, *Republic*, trans. Robin Waterfield (Oxford: Oxford University Press, 1993): 159-63, 168-70, 174, 183.
2. Quotations from: "She Craves Not Spring for Herself Alone: Marx, Engels, Lenin and Mao on the Liberation of Women," *Revolutionary Worker* #948 (March 15, 1998); at http://rwor.org/a/v19/940-49/948/quotes.htm (7/23/03).
3. Charlotte Perkins Gilman, *Herland* [1915], chapter 7; found at http://www.fantasticfiction.co.uk/etexts/n4558_7.htm (7/23/03).
4. Charlotte Perkins Gilman, *Women and Economics: A Study of the Economic Relations Between Men and Women as a Factor in Social Evolution*, ed. Carl N. Degler (New York: Harper & Row, 1966 [1898]): 270-94.
5. Aldous Huxley, *Brave New World* (New York and Evanston: Harper & Row, 1946 [1932]): 26, 44, 175.
6. Arthur W. Calhoun, *A Social History of the American Family* (New York: Barnes & Noble, 1945 [1918]): 171-72.
7. From: *Recent Social Trends in the United States: Report of the President's Research Committee on Social Trends* (New York: McGraw-Hill, 1933): 661-678. Emphasis added.
8. See: George Herbert Mead, *Mind, Self, and Society* (Chicago: University of Chicago Press, 1934).
9. On these early decades, see: Margaret O'Brien Steinfels, *Who's Minding the Children? The History and Politics of Day Care in America* (New York: Simon & Schuster, 1973); and Bernard Greenblatt, *Responsibility for Child Care: The Changing Role of Family and State in Child Development* (San Francisco: Jossey-Bass, 1977): 41-69.

10. Letter, Alva Myrdal to Bertil Hammer, Sept. 15, 1929, Alva Myrdal Letter Collection, Labor Movement Archive, Stockholm.
11. From materials in the Alva Myrdal Archive (*AMA*), Labor Movement Archive, Stockholm, files 3.000 and 4.000.
12. *AMA* 5.200, 5.500, and 6.202-1.
13. Alva Myrdal, "Kollektiv bostadsform," *Tiden* 24 (Dec. 1932): 602.
14. Alva Myrdal, "Yrkes-kvinnans barn," *Yrkes-kvinnor klubbnytt* (Feb. 1933): 63; also *AMA* 6.201.
15. The full story is told in: Allan Carlson, *The Swedish Experiment in Family Politics: The Myrdals and the Interwar Population Crisis* (New Brunswick, NJ: Transaction Publishers, 1990).
16. Statens Offentliga Utredningen 1938:47, *Betänkande angående gift kvinnas försvärvsarbete m.m.* (Stockholm, 1938): and Alva Myrdal, *Nation and Family* (New York: Harper & Brothers, 1941): 218-23.
17. Alva Myrdal, *Stadsbarn: En boken deras föstran i storbarnkammare* (Stockholm: Koopertiva förbundets bokförlag, 1935). On gender-neutral play and the re-engineering of gender roles, see also: Alva Myrdal, *Riktiga leksaker* ["Proper Playthings"] (Stockholm: Koopertiva förbundets bokförlag, 1936).
18. Brita Åkerman, "Goda grannar på 1920-talet och på 70-talet," *Att bo* (June 1973): 21; and Sven Wallander, *Minnen. Del 1: HSBs öden från 1920-talet till 1957* (Stockholm: HSB:s Riksförbund, 1965): 100-01.
19. Yvonne Hirdman, "The Importance of Gender in the Swedish Labor Movement, Or: A Swedish Dilemma." Paper prepared for the Swedish National Institute of Working Life, 2002: 3-5.
20. On the Second Commission, see: Ann Katrin Hatje, *Befolkningsfrågan och välfärden: debatten om familjepolitik och nativitetsökning under 1930- och 1940-talen* (Stockholm: Allmänna förlaget, 1974). More broadly, see: Barbara Hobson, "Feminist Strategies and Gendered Discourses in Welfare States: Married Women's Right to Work in the United States and Sweden," in Seth Koren and Sonya Michel, eds., *Mothers of a New World: Maternalist Politics and the Origins of Welfare States* (New York and London: Routledge, 1993): 396-429.
21. "Historical Origins of Child Care Politics: The United States and Sweden" prepared by The David and and Lucille Packard Foundation, at: http://www.futureofchildren.org/information2827/information_show.htm?doc_id=77721 (7/21/03).
22. Anita Nyberg, "From Foster Mothers to Child Care Center: A History of Working Mothers and Child Care in Sweden," *Feminist Economics* 6 (No. 1, 2000): 15.
23. A point acknowledged in: Dorothy McBride Stetson and Amy Maxur, eds., *Comparative State Feminisms* (Thousand Oaks, CA: SAGE Publications, 1995): 241.
24. On this latter change, see: Ron Lesthaeghe, "A Century of Demographic and Cultural Change in Western Europe: An Exploration of Underlying Dimensions," *Population and Development Review* 9 (No. 3, 1983): 429.
25. These labels all come from Hirdman, "The Importance of Gender in the Swedish Labor Movement," pp. 8-9, 11.
26. *Jämlikhet-första rapporten från SAP-LO:s arbetsgrupp för jämlikhetsfrågan* (Stockholm: Prisma, 1969): 102.
27. *SAP Congress Minutes, 1972*, p. 759, in Hirdman, "The Importance of Gender in the Swedish Labor Movement," p. 6.
28. Nyberg, "From Foster Mothers to Child Care Centers," pp. 15-16.
29. Hirdman, "The Importance of Gender in the Swedish Labor Movement," p. 10. Emphasis added.

30.   An earlier version is also offered in: Allan Carlson, *Family Questions: Reflections on the American Social Crisis* (New Brunswick, NJ: Transaction Publishers, 1988): 3-15.

31.   See: Allan Carlson, "'Sanctif[ying] the Traditional Family': The New Deal and National Solidarity," *The Family in America* 16 (Jan.-Feb., 2002): 1-16.

32.   See: Frances Fox Piven, "Ideology and the State: Women, Power and the Welfare State," in Linda Gordon, ed., *Woman, the State and Welfare* (Madison, WI: University of Wisconsin Press, 1990): 251-64.

33.   Jane Lewis, "Gender and Welfare Regimes: Further Thoughts," *Social Politics* 4 (Summer 1997): 172.

34.   Stanley Greenspan, *The Growth of the Mind: The Endangered Origins of Intelligence* (New York: Addison-Wesley, 1996).

35.   George P. Murdoch, *Social Structure* (New York: The Free Press, 1949): 7-8.

36.   C. Owen Lovejoy, "The Origin of Man," *Science* 211 (1981): 341-50.

37.   Lewis, "Gender and Welfare Regimes," p. 173.

38.   For a recent survey of this evidence, see: Bryce Christensen, "Breeding Little Monsters: How Day Care is Exposing America's Children to Unnatural Plagues," *The Family in America* 16 (June 2002): 1-8.

39.   Jan Hoem, "Social Policy and Recent Fertility Change in Sweden," *Population Review* 16 (December 1990): 735-48.

40.   Ron Lesthaeghe and Dominique Meekers, "Value Changes and the Dimensions of Familism in the European Community," *European Journal of Population* 2 (1986): 260.

41.   John Ermisch, "The Economic Environment for Family Formation," in David Coleman, ed., *Europe's Population in the 1990s* (Oxford: Oxford University Press, 1990): 159.

42.   Heather Joshi, "Projections of European Population Decline: Serious Demography or False Alarm?" in Coleman, *Europe's Population in the 1990s*, p. 263.

43.   *Statistical Abstract of the United States: 2002* (Washington, DC: U.S. Census Bureau, 2002): Table 550.

44.   Reported in: Bridget Maher, ed., *The Family Portrait* (Washington, DC: Family Research Council, 2002): 49.

4

Reinventing the Schoolroom:
Education as Homecoming

Partisans of "school choice" were cheered recently by reports of success from an unexpected place: Sweden. The inaugural issue of *School Choice: Issues in Thought*, published by the Milton and Rose D. Friedman Foundation, celebrates the results of that Scandinavian land's 1992 education reform. The measure requires municipalities to fund independent schools on terms equal to existing state schools. It also allows parents to choose which school their children will attend. To qualify for funding, independent schools have to be approved by a National Agency for Education, meet educational standards and targets set by the state system, and be open to all children regardless of their ability, religion, or ethnic origin. These independent schools cannot charge extra tuition. Nonetheless, by 2002, the number of such institutions had grown from 122 to 637. Four percent of primary school children and 5.6 percent of secondary school pupils nationwide were now in independent schools, up from about one percent in the pre-reform period. The innovation proved to be popular with teachers and apparently had no measurable negative effects on the state schools.[1]

All the same, there are some curiosities about the Swedish results. To begin with, so-called "confessional" schools played only "a minor part" in the reform, although they were fully eligible to participate. Some Muslim schools appeared among immigrant communities, but the number of Christian schools—already small—did not grow at all. Instead, most of the new independent schools were created by for-profit corporations and offered special curricula such as Montessori and Steiner-Waldorf. In turn, these new schools tended to be located in the more affluent parts of the larger Swedish cities.

Moreover, although the reform began in 1992 at the initiative of a center-right coalition government, it also won the support of the leadership of the leftist Social Democratic Labor Party, which returned to its traditional political dominance in 1994. As noted in the prior chapter, these Social Democrats have since 1968 pursued a consistent policy aimed at dismantling the family. The Party has intentionally eliminated the legal, economic, and cultural bases for marriage. It has largely dismantled parental authority and encouraged children's rights. The Party's sexual policies favor early experimentation, universal contraception, homosexual rights, and cohabitation.[2] School choice, it appears, has at least not proven incompatible with this larger social agenda.

Accordingly, the Swedish example usefully clarifies some issues regarding educational reform. Because of the exercise of a limited consumer choice, the encouragement to a kind of state-funded entrepreneurship, and the lack of any guiding moral vision, the twenty-first-century libertarian can celebrate this experiment in "school choice." Because the results pose no threat to Sweden's intentionally post-family social-political order and may actually divert energy from more important issues, the modern socialist can embrace "school choice" as well. It appears that only the social conservative, normally an advocate for parental authority, is left to ask several nagging questions: Is shared moral purpose truly no longer possible? Do not the local community and the inherited culture also have claims on the child? Are not the family virtues the starting place for real learning? And: Might there still be ways to reconcile parental autonomy with communitarian claims?

The Grim Roots of "Common Schools"

I hasten to note that these family- and community-centered questions need not require "the public schools as we know them" as answers. Indeed, the record of American state education regarding the status and role of the family is fairly dismal, with one remarkable time period as exception.

From the very beginning, public school advocates aimed—as they had to—at undermining and displacing the family as the center of children's lives. The most important claim for public education was that only a compulsory system of this sort could unify a scattered and diverse people: the parochial ideas of families obviously stood in the way. Benjamin Rush, perhaps the most radical of the signers of the Declaration of Independence, urged a politically-charged vision of learning that began by demoting the family:

> Our country includes family, friends, and property, and [the state] should be preferred to them all. Let our pupil be taught to love his family, but let him be taught at the same time that he must forsake and even forget them when the welfare of his country requires it.[3]

Horace Mann of Massachusetts, the acknowledged "father" of the Common Schools in the mid-nineteenth century, held similar attitudes. Citing the "neglect," ignorance, and inefficiencies of families in his state, he underscored the special brutality of what he labeled "monster families," deemed totally unworthy of their children. Indeed, Mann linked the "common school" system to a vision of the later welfare state, where government simply assumed the *role of parent*. As he wrote in his school report for 1846: "Massachusetts is *parental* in her government. More and more, as year after year rolls by, she seeks to substitute prevention for remedy, and rewards for penalties."[4]

The *Common School Journal*, founded by Mann and colleagues in 1838, featured the deconstruction of family life as one of its regular themes. Passages included:

- The public schools succeed because "parents, although the most sunken in depravity themselves, welcome the proposals and receive with gratitude the services of…moral philanthropy in behalf of their families";[5]
- "[T]hese are…illustrations of the folly of a parent, who interferes with and perplexes a teacher while instructing or training his child";[6]
- "the little interests or conveniences of the family" must be subordinate to "the paramount subject" of the school;[7] and
- "there are many worthless parents."[8]

Such sentiments spread with public education across the country over the middle decades of the nineteenth century. John Swett, an early superintendent of the California state schools, was blunt in his opinion that the state must supplant the family. In his 1864 Report to the state legislature, Swett explained that "the child should be taught to consider his instructor…superior to the parent in point of authority…The vulgar impression that parents have a legal right to dictate to teachers is entirely erroneous.… Parents have no remedy as against the teacher."[9]

F. W. Parker, the so-called "father of progressive education" and inspiration for John Dewey, told the 1895 convention of the National Education Association (NEA) that "The child is not in school for knowledge. He is there to live, and to put his life, nurtured in the school, into the community." The family home and religious faith simply must give way to a grander vision. As Parker concluded: "Every *school* in the land should be a *home* and *heaven* for children."[10]

State Schools and Family Decay

In fact, there is *direct* evidence of a *strong* linkage between the *spread* of mass state education and the *decline* of the family. It comes from the field of demography and uses fertility as a measure of family commitment.

Demographer John Caldwell's *Theory of Fertility Decline* appeared in 1982,[11] and represents a provocative attempt to apply anthropological research, primarily in Africa and Australia, across the board. Caldwell notes, as others have before, that fertility declines only when there is a change in economic relations within the family. In agrarian societies, for example, children are economic assets and fertility is high while in industrial societies the economic value of the young turns negative and fertility declines.

But in an important turn of the argument, Caldwell emphasizes that it is not the rise of cities or industry, per se, that causes this change in family relations. Rather, he shows that it is the *prior* introduction of new ideas through *mass state education* that stimulates the critical shift in the parent-child relation. He argues that state-mandated schooling serves as the driving force behind the turn in preference from a large to a small family and the re-engineering of the family into an entity limited in its claims.

Evidence from the United States gives strong support to Caldwell's emphasis on mass state schooling as a major explanation of family decline. The steady fall in American fertility between 1850 and 1900 has long puzzled demographers, for throughout this era the United States remained predominantly rural and absorbed a steady flow of young immigrants, circumstances normally associated with large families. Caldwell's interpreters[12] speculated, though, that the leadership role of the United States in introducing a mass state education system might explain the change. And indeed, U.S. data from 1871 to 1900 show a *remarkably strong negative relationship* between the fertility of women and an index of public school growth developed by L. P. Ayres in 1920. Fertility decline was particularly related to the average number of days that children attended public school in a given year. Even among rural farming families, where children still held economic value, the negative influence of public schooling on fertility was clear. Each additional month that rural children spent in school decreased family size in that district by .23 children. Indeed, we see here how state education quite literally "consumed" children, and weakened families.

Norman Ryder of Princeton University agrees that mass state education disrupts family integrity.[13] He writes approvingly in *The Population Bulletin of the United Nations*: "Education of the junior generation is a subversive influence. Boys who go to school distinguish between what they learn there and what their father can teach them.... The reinforcement of the [family] control structure is undermined when the young are trained outside the family for specialized roles in which the father has no competence."[14] The broader contest is between the home and the centralizing state for the allegiance of the child. As Ryder puts it: "Political organizations, like economic organizations, demand loyalty and attempt to neutralize family particularism. There is a struggle between the family and the State for the minds of the young." In this struggle, the state school serves as "the chief instrument for teaching [a new] citizenship, in a direct appeal to the children over the heads of their parents." The school also serves as the medium for communicating "state morality" and a state mythology designed to displace those of families.[15]

Ryder's work underscores the vital importance of *specific functions* to family institutional strength. For example, when families educate their own children, serve as the focus of religious life, and raise the largest share of their own food, the persons in these families are more likely to fix their first loyalties on the home. When these functions pass over to rival institutions, families lose these claims and diminish as institutions. Using solid empirical evidence, then, we actually can indict *public* education as a *direct* cause of family decline.

The First Pro-Family Movement

The exception to this record came in the early decades of the twentieth century. American family life did show at that time many signs of increasing disorder. Between 1890 and 1920, the number of divorced Americans rose three-fold. Meanwhile, the U.S. birth-rate fell by about a third. Alongside the already examined effects of public education on these numbers, there were other new idea systems leveling attacks on the natural family: equity feminism, which labeled the mother-at-home as "a parasite on society;" neo-Malthusianism, which linked poverty to fertility, condemned large families, and urged the universal adoption of birth control; and cultural relativism, which held that it was impossible to find common cultural values or a shared "way of life" in the teeming diversity of immigrant America.[16]

Responding to these challenges, there rose what we might call America's first conscious pro-family movement. Prominent figures were actually in its ranks, notably President Theodore Roosevelt. He called "easy divorce...a *bane* to any nation, a *curse* to society, a *menace* to the home, [and] an *incitement* to married unhappiness, and to immorality."[17] He argued that no nation could "exist at all" unless its average woman was "the home-keeper, the good wife, and unless she is the mother of a sufficient number of healthy children" to keep the nation "going forward."[18]

Another family advocate of that era, Frances Kellor, served as director of Americanization Work for the Federal Bureau of Education. She concluded that the key to turning immigrants into Americans lay within the home. All women, native born and immigrant alike, had a common identity as nurturers and "a common gift for caring." She argued: "If we start with the family and work upward, we get a sound city that will stand the strain of any crisis because its weakest links are strong.... Approached from the neighborhood and family and met squarely, the problem of Americanization can be solved adequately."[19] National unity, Kellor implied, could be built on "one motherhood from diversely situated women," with training in homemaking being the "fulcrum" of Americanization.[20]

Meanwhile, Liberty Hyde Bailey, the famed dean of the College of Agriculture at Cornell University, argued that family renewal required the revitalization of rural life. Remember that at this time Americans still saw themselves as a farming people. Dean Bailey argued that, given the low urban birthrates, "the farm home assumes a most important relation to civilization," furnishing new life for both countryside and city. "The farm home also carries an obligation to maintain the quality of the population. It is a preservator of morals." And yet, Bailey continued, "while the home is the center or pivot of our civilization, it is the last thing to be taught in schools."[21] Looking to the cities, the prominent labor activist Florence Kelley agreed: "The schools may truthfully be said actively to divert the little girls from homelife...[offering] wretched preparation for home making."[22] Through his position as chairman of President Roosevelt's National Commission on Country-Life, Bailey resolved that "the home-making phase of country-life is as important as the field-farming phase" and that the teaching of "home-economics" or "home making"—"the whole round of woman's work and place"—was essential to rebuilding American families and civilization.[23]

Two major federal policy actions followed. The Smith-Lever Act of 1914 created the Extension program of the U.S. Department of Agriculture, charged with teaching modern farming techniques to men and boys and homemaking and housekeeping to women and girls. The Smith-Hughes Act came three years later. Representing *the first federal program* providing *direct aid* to elementary and secondary schools, Smith-Hughes granted money for teacher training and salaries in the fields of agriculture, the industrial arts, and home-making.

These innovations fell onto receptive soil. Despite the centralizing dreams of Horace Mann and his successors, the public schools still showed, circa 1920, a great diversity and a residual, locally grounded social conservatism that welcomed efforts to strengthen families. Indeed, as late as 1932, there were still 127,531 independent school districts in the United States; many of them operating but a single school. The great push for school consolidation was still to come. And, of course, the new federal money for teachers was welcomed, too, with little appreciation for the unhealthy precedent being set.

Clearly, the model for family renewal embodied in these federal measures was the breadwinning husband and father operating a small farm or shop or earning a "family wage" in the city and married to a fulltime, "home-making" wife and mother. As Alba Bales of North Dakota State University explained in 1923: "[Young women] must have the training and assurance which will help them see that the house is built right for her as a housekeeper and household manager."[24] Efficiency and informed consumption in homemaking would be stressed. Yet the true spirit of this federal experiment in family renewal was best captured by two songs found in the Extension Service's *4-H Songbook* of 1928. For boys, "The Plowing Song":

> A growing day in a waking field
> And a furrow straight and long
> A golden sun and a lifting breeze,
> And we follow with a song.
> Sons of the soil are we,
> Lads of the field and flock.
> Turning our sods, asking no odds;
> Where is a life so free?
> Sons of the soil are we,
> Men of the coming years;
> Facing the dawn, brain ruling brawn.
> Lords of our lands we'll be!

And for the girls, the song "Dreaming" (here, the third verse):

> My home must have its mother,
> May I grow sweet and wise;
> My home must have its father,
> With honor in his eyes;
> My home must have its children,
> God grant the parents grace—
> To keep our home through all the years,
> A kindly, happy place.

Again, this was federally engineered education, circa 1928, a far cry, say, from the sexually egalitarian spirit of today's Title IX. Indeed, it almost seems to rise out of an alternate moral universe. But this family-building experiment worked, at least for a time. Small-scale family agriculture was not saved, but the ethos of homemaking survived, with a strong influence on the generation coming of age in the 1940s. With federal backing, there was a vast increase in the number of home economics teachers. Homemaking classes for the girls in food preparation, sewing, and home management grew ubiquitous, in rural and city districts alike. In 1945, the Future Homemakers of America (FHA) organized and this high school club soon claimed over 600,000 members. Home economics joined elementary education as the most popular major for young women in college. And there were surely results; the marriage boom of the 1940s and 1950s, the better-known Baby Boom, and the new domesticity of the Suburban Boom all reflected—and at some level may have been stimulated by—this home-building educational work, actively encouraged by Uncle Sam.

But the renewed American family did not last. While many factors were involved in this failure, one certainly was the political and
intellectual collapse of the home economics discipline and of the
"homemaker/breadwinner" family model that it sustained. Amendments in *1963*—a critical year in so many ways!—to the old Smith-
Hughes Act *reduced* funding for homemaking and family-life education and *required*, for the first time, that *home ec* teachers also
train their students for gainful employment outside the home. Indeed, the spread of feminist ideology soon shook home economics
to its core, a shock reflected in the very name of the discipline. By
1970, five new labels for the relevant school department were in
use; by 1990, over seventy-five. These new names included "human ecology," "human development," "consumer sciences," "contemporary living," and "life studies." The only word that never appeared among these innovations was "home," a concept now fraught
with embarrassment.[25] Congress mercifully killed the Smith-Hughes
Act in 1997, its animating spirit long since gone.

Perhaps there were internal weaknesses to the "home economics"
doctrine, as well. By bringing the logic of industry, of consumerism,
and of the quest for efficiency into the family circle, perhaps home
economists set in motion processes that eventually undid their own
work.

Public Schools: Back to the Roots

Public education, in any case, eagerly and easily returned to its
more natural stance athwart the family. Title IX of the Education
Amendments of 1972 prohibited discrimination on the basis of sex
in all programs receiving federal funds, driving a final nail in the
coffin of the sexual division of labor that had undergirded the renewed American family. School consolidation speeded up: there were
only 17,995 school districts left by 1990, a decline of 85 percent
since 1932. This loss of local control was complemented by a cen-
tralization of power in groups such as the National Education Association, institutions with a special animus toward the family model
so recently celebrated. By the early 1980s, the NEA vigorously attacked "materials that promote sex stereotypes" such as non-em-
ployed mothers and breadwinning fathers and affirmed the right of
school children "to live in an environment of freely available information, knowledge, and wisdom about sexuality." Once again,

"multiculturalism" must serve as the vehicle for national unity.[26] More recent resolutions condemn "homophobia," celebrate "reproductive freedom" and "family planning" in the schools, welcome "diverse sexual orientation," and urge the positive portrayal "of the roles and contributions of gay, lesbian, and bisexual people throughout history."[27] Prominent educators again speak openly and contemptuously about the "racial, religious, ethnic, sexist, and economic stereotyping" that parents presumably give to their children.[28] The founding spirit of Horace Mann and *The Common School Journal* hath returned and while it is probably flustered by all the sex talk, this spirit must heartily approve of the fresh verbal flagellations given to parents.

But is not "school choice," via tax credits, vouchers, and charter schools, the logical response? As a step in challenging the existing centralized monopoly, "school choice" initiatives could have a positive effect. But, particularly for people of religious faith, there are haunting voices posing those deeper questions touching on educational purpose, the claims of culture and community, and the values that must bind a people together. The Kentucky poet, novelist, and essayist Wendell Berry points to the strange values of modern education:

> According to the new norm, the child's destiny is not to succeed the parents, but to outmode them…. The schools are no longer oriented to a cultural inheritance that it is their duty to pass on unimpaired, but to the career, which is to say the future of the child…. He or she is educated to leave home and earn money in a provisional future that has nothing to do with place or community…. It is no wonder that, under these circumstances, "educators" tend to look upon parents as bad influences and wish to take the children away from home as soon as possible. And many parents, in truth, are now finding their children an encumbrance at home, where there is no useful work for them to do, and are glad enough to turn them over to the state for the use of the future.[29]

These are the symptoms of a pervasive *homelessness*, one vastly broader in scope than the "homeless problem" normally discussed in the media and one deserving our close attention. The Christian scholars Steven Bouma-Prediger and Brian Walsh emphasize that true education "must engender an ethos of intimacy and affection," one rooted in a geographically defined community such as village or neighborhood, where "for the sake of Christian discipleship, we must secede from the empire that has rendered us homeless."[30] Social analyst Bryce Christensen describes home as "a place sanctified by the abiding ties of wedlock, parenthood, and family obligation; a place demanding sacrifice and devotion but promising loving care and warm acceptance," a place anchored in turn in a specific geographic locale.[31] And nature educator Wes Jackson asks whether schools ought now be offering a new major in "homecoming."[32]

True Homecoming

Moving beyond the strict mechanics of "school choice," what might contemporary education for "home building" and "homecoming" look like?

The first principle is that all true and lasting efforts must flow from the primal or natural social units: families; villages; neighborhoods; faith communities. An effective long-term "education in homecoming" cannot be imposed from the top, down. This was the mistake of the Smith-Hughes Act. Federally-directed mass education in "industrialized breadwinning" for the boys and "commercialized homemaking" for the girls showed impressive results for a generation, but then crumbled swiftly from internal deficiencies and external ideological challenges. True "education in homecoming" will instead flow upward from the familial and spiritual foundations of the good society.

Similarly, "national unity" will not be won by the imposition from above of a new cultural ideology of either "multiculturalism" or some reminted version of Anglo-Saxon "Americanism." For the whole of the last century, the effective unifying metaphors of "the American Way of life" have come instead from the discovery of common affection for marriage, family, and place—affections that transcend religious and ethnic divisions, and affections that also grow from the family home as the cell of society.[33]

Allow me to illustrate this big idea with a little story. Several years ago, I participated in a debate over children's issues on Wisconsin Public Radio, and at one point noted something positive about home schooling. Another panelist, a professor of social work at the University of Wisconsin-Madison, responded sternly. Given all the new immigrants coming to America, she said, *only* the public schools could craft a necessary degree of public unity. "It was the values found in the McGuffey Readers that unified this nation," she concluded. With the gleam of the successful trapper in my eye, I responded: "If you can show me one public schoolroom in this state where the McGuffey Readers are used today, I will concede your point. But I know that you cannot. For you see, the state of Wisconsin's education regulations specifically *ban* the McGuffey Readers from use, because of their moralistic content. However, I could show you dozens, even hundreds, of home school classrooms in Wisconsin where McGuffey is alive, well, and in use." Unlike the state schools, you see, these homes were—and are—still building respect for a unifying public morality.

Indeed, the most obvious path toward education as homecoming lies in these home schools. Here we find families engaged in a fundamental revolution, *recovering* a *vital* family function lost to the aggressive state a century-and-a-half earlier. With over two million children now involved, home school families are *reinventing* American education. The direct effects are becoming well known, and are broadly impressive. In grades one through four, according to a University of Maryland study, median test scores for home-schooled children are a full grade above those of public *and* private school students. By grade eight, the median scores of home schoolers are almost *four* grade equivalents above those of their peers in public *and* private schools.[34] The *domination* of national spelling and geography bees by home schoolers in recent years testifies as well to the ability of family-centered education to motivate extraordinary individual accomplishment.

Relative to homecoming, though, the more important traits of home schooling may be the social and familial. Simply put, home education empowers "homemaking" families. According to one recent survey, over *97 percent* of home school students had parents who were married, compared to a 72 percent figure nationwide. *Sixty-two* percent of home schooling families had three or more children, compared to a mere 20 percent of the nationwide sample. A full *third* (33.5 percent) of home-schooled families actually had four or more children, over against six percent nationwide. Meanwhile, 77 percent of home schooling mothers did *not* work for pay, compared to only 30 percent nationwide. And of the 23 percent of home schooling mothers who did work, the vast majority (86.3 percent) did so only part-time. These are clearly home-building women and child rich families.[35]

How might public policy encourage home education? Home schooling is now legal, with varying degrees of regulation, in all fifty states. The model statute may be Alaska's, where the state's Compulsory Education Law simply and fully exempts from coverage any child who "is being educated in the child's home by a parent or legal guardian."[36] This freedom precludes registration, reporting, or curricular requirements. In Illinois, home schoolers can claim an Education Tax Credit of 20 percent on educational expenses, up to $500. Reflecting the same principle, tax-free federal education savings accounts and proposed education tax credits should be made larger still and available for all learning expenses, not just tuition.

Private and religious schools can also be centers for education as homecoming. The key here is deep parental involvement in the operation of the schools. The best ones are those built on a clear—and usually religious—moral vision and on the work, sacrifice, and treasure of parents and students. While acknowledging the potential of universal state vouchers to advance "school choice," I am still wary of them for two reasons. First, the potential for regulatory intrusion by state authorities here is real. Relative to the goal of "homecoming," this could take the form of anti-family gender-role engineering (perhaps under the broad spirit of Title IX) that would undermine effective "homebuilding." Second, the availability of vouchers would lessen—perhaps dramatically—the spirit of family sacrifice and the personal parental involvement that animate the best independent schools.

Instead, I would urge the steady expansion of general child-sensitive tax measures, such as the personal exemption and the child tax credit on the federal income tax. As a minimum, the child exemption and the child tax credit should each be doubled; for real tax equity, they should then be doubled again. To give "choice" to families with relatively little income and tax liability, the expanded child tax credit could be made fully refundable.

In addition, a strong case can be made for treating *all* educational expenses as tax deductible. Investments in physical capital by businesses currently enjoy favored treatment under tax policy: deductibility in some cases; generous depreciation tables in others. As an investment in *human capital*, educational costs should logically enjoy similar treatment: full deductibility.

This focus on tax benefits would prevent regulatory intrusion and spare independent schools from the loss of their peculiar and—I believe—necessary energy.

What then about the public schools, which still embrace the great majority of American children? Here, I craft a still greater dream and return to a recommendation I first made over twenty years ago: We should *move toward* a "radical *de*consolidation of the public system, down even to the single-school level," which would weaken "bureaucratic and union strangleholds on the schools and so return them to [real] community control, where parental and neighborhood moral judgements could again play a role."[37] This goal or process would rest on the finding, phrased in Bill Kauffman's words, that "every promise of the consolidationists is, at best, an exaggeration, at worst, a lie."[38] Not efficiency, nor improved outcomes, nor greater social equity have been gained. Moving beyond "charter schools," this deconsolidationist approach would come full circle and reground tax-supported schools in their places: their neighborhoods. Each school would have its own elected governing board, and its own tax levy. Where the economic circumstances of a school district were inadequate, a state education board could make a supplemental grant out of general revenues. High school districts could draw students from several independent primary districts.

The use of busing and magnet schools to prevent or reverse racial segregation would admittedly come to an end under this approach. However, recent reports from the Civil Rights Project of Harvard University have found American schools *more* segregated in 2002 than they were thirty years earlier when court-ordered busing first came into its own.[39] *Hundreds* of *billions* of dollars have been squandered in this campaign. It is time to end this wasteful, fruitless, and degrading exercise in social engineering and turn instead to building viable neighborhoods resting on good local schools.

Most importantly, these neighborhood, village, or township schools would be "open." Like a community college, they would *offer* their learning and extracurricular opportunities to *all students* in the district, *but would compel none*. Some families might choose a complete school day; others just a science or math class; still others, only choir or the soccer team. The local school would have a strong incentive to *serve* the neighborhood and its inhabitants, rather than to force them along a one-curriculum-fits-all path. Once again, school boards could be expected to reflect and respect neighborhood values and sensibilities. The school should become the focus and pride of the neighborhood, village, or township, so helping to unite all people—public schoolers, private schoolers, home schoolers, and the childless alike—with their special place on earth. For those relatively rare cases of complete parental abdication of educational responsibility, "child neglect" laws would come into play. In all these ways, parental autonomy would finally be reconciled with the claims of local culture and community. And by building on strengthened families and neighborhoods, we would be crafting the greater strength of the nation.

These are, I believe, the ways of achieving *a true homecoming* for America's schools, families, and children.

Notes

1. Fredrik Bergstrom and F. Mikael Sandstrom, "School Choice Works! The Case of Sweden," *School Choice: Issues in Thought* 1 (Dec. 2002): 1-26.
2. See: Allan Carlson, *The Swedish Experiment in Family Politics: The Myrdals and the Interwar Population Crisis* (New Brunswick, NJ: Transaction Publishers, 1990): chapter 7; and David Popenoe, *Disturbing the Nest: Family Change and Decline in Modern Societies* (New York: Aldine de Gruyter, 1988).
3. Benjamin Rush, "Plan for the Establishment of Public Schools [1786]," reprinted in Frederick Rudolph, ed., *Essays on Education in the Early Republic* (Cambridge, MA: Belknap Press of Harvard University, 1965): 14.
4. See: Horace Mann, "Challenges to a New Age [1845]," in Lewis Filler, ed., *Horace Mann on the Crisis of Education* (Yellow Springs, OH: The Antioch Press, 1965): 86; and Horace Mann, "The Ground of the Free School System [1846]," in *Old South Leaflets* No. 109 (Boston, MA: Old South Meeting House, 1902): 12-18.
5. Dr. Chalmers, "The Power of Education," *The Common School Journal* 3 (September 1, 1841): 269.
6. "Duty of Parents to Cooperate with Teachers," *The Common School Journal* 8 (August 1, 1846): 226.
7. Horace Mann, "Fourth Annual Report of the Secretary of the Board of Education," *The Common School Journal* 3 (December 1, 1841): 359.
8. "Extract from the Christian Review for March, 1841," *The Common School Journal* 3 (May 1, 1841): 143.
9. John Swett, *History of the Public School System of California* (San Francisco: Bancroft, 1876): 115.
10. Francis Wayland Parker, "Response," *N.E.A. Journal*, 1895, p. 62; in Rousas John Rushdoony, *The Messianic Character of American Education* (Philadelphia: Presbyterian and Reformed Publishing Co., 1963): 104.
11. John C. Caldwell, *Theory of Fertility Decline* (New York: Academic Press, 1982): particularly chapters 4 and 10.
12. Avery M. Guest and Stewart E. Tolnay, "Children's Roles and Fertility: Late Nineteenth Century United States," *Social Science History* 7 (1983): 355-80.
13. Norman Ryder, "Fertility and Family Structure," *Population Bulletin of the United Nations* 15 (1983): 18-32.
14. Ryder, "Fertility and Family Structure," p.29.
15. Ibid., pp. 29-30.
16. Regarding the latter, see: Horace Kallen, "Democracy versus the Melting Pot. Part I," pp. 192-93 and "Part II," pp. 217-20 in *The Nation* 106 (Feb. 18 and Feb. 25, 1915).
17. Theodore Roosevelt, *The Works of Theodore Roosevelt: Memorial Edition* (New York: Charles Scribner's Sons, 1924): Vol. XVIII, p. 231; and Vol. XXII, p. 594.
18. Theodore Roosevelt, *Works*, Vol. XVII, p. 228.

19.   Frances A. Kellor, *Neighborhood Americanization: A Discussion of the Alien in a New Country and of the Native American in His Home Country.* An address to the Colony Club in New York City, Feb. 8, 1918; in Wisconsin State Historical Society Pamphlet Collection, # 54-997.

20.   From Gwendoyln Mink, *The Wages of Motherhood: Inequality in the Welfare State, 1917-1942* (Ithaca and London: Cornell University Press, 1994): 9, 25.

21.   Liberty Hyde Bailey, *The Training of Farmers* (New York: The Century Co., 1909): 71, 238.

22.   In Molly Ladd-Taylor, *Mother-Work: Women, Child Welfare, and the State, 1890-1930* (Urbana, IL: University of Illinois Press, 1994): 100.

23.   Liberty Hyde Bailey, *The Country-Life Movement in the United States* (New York: The Macmillion Co., [1911] 1920): 63-65, 93-95.

24.   "History of Alba Bales House," at http://www.lib.ndsu.nodak.edu/archives/ndsubuildings/Alba.Bales/AlbaBalesHistory.html.

25.   E. Haley, R. S. Peggram, and C. J. Ley, "Enhancing Program Viability," *Journal of Home Economics* 85 (Fall 1993).

26.   "NEA Resolutions," *Today's Education* (1982-83 Annual): 151-87.

27.   "Resolutions of the National Education Association Concerning Sexual Diversity Orientation" at http://www.afaga.org/NEA.htm; and "Some NEA Resolutions Passed at 2002 Convention in Dallas," at http://www.eagleforum.org/educate/2002/aug02/NEA-Resolutions.shtml.

28.   See: Robert S. Wicks, *Morality and the Schools* (Washington, DC: Council for Basic Education, 1981): 7.

29.   Wendell Berry, *What Are People For?* (San Francisco: North Point Press, 1990): 162-64.

30.   Steven Bouma-Prediger and Brian Walsh, "Education for Homelessness or Home-making? The Christian College in a Postmodern Culture," a paper presented at the conference, "Christian Scholarship—for What?" Calvin College, September 28, 2001, pp. 17-18.

31.   Bryce Christensen, "Homeless in America," *The Family in America* 17 (Jan. 2003): 2.

32.   Wes Jackson, *Becoming Native to This Place* (Washington, DC: Counterpoint, 1996): 97.

33.   This is the theme of my book: Allan Carlson, *The "American Way": Family and Community in the Shaping of the American Identity* (Wilmington, DE: ISI Books, 2003).

34.   Lawrence M. Rudner, "Scholastic Achievement and Demographic Characteristics of Home School Students in 1998," *Education Policy Analysis Archives* 7 (23 Mar. 1999): 19.

35.   Rudner, "Scholastic Achievement and Demographic Characteristics of Home School Students in 1998," pp. 7-8, 12.

36.   Alaska State Education Statute, Chapter 14.30 Pupils and Educational Programs for Pupils. Article 01. Compulsory Education Sec. 14.30.010. Adopted September 7, 1997.

37.   Allan C. Carlson, "The Rotting Core of the American Experiment...And a Possible Cure," *Persuasion at Work* 4 (Dec. 1983): 5.

38.   Bill Kauffman, "Weatherbeaten Shacks, Ignorant Parents: What's Behind School Consolidation?" *The Family in America* 10 (April 1996): 5.

39.   Gary Orfield, "Schools More Separate: Consequences of a Decade of Resegregation," The Civil Rights Project of Harvard University, 17 July 2001; and Gary Orfield, Erica Frankenberg, and Chungmei Lee, "A Multiracial Society with Segregated Schools: Are We Losing the Dream?" The Civil Rights Project of Harvard University, Feb. 20, 2003.

5

"Bailey Park" or "Greater Pottersville"? The Natural Family in the Twenty-First-Century Suburb

It's A Wonderful Life, the modest 1946 film that has become an American icon, offers rival images of the mid-twentieth-century American suburb. In one scene, George and Mary Bailey drive the immigrant Martini family from its miserable shack in Potter's Field to a new ranch-style house in the Bailey Park development. "I own my own home!" shouts Mr. Martini, as Mary Bailey presents the family with welcoming gifts of salt, wine, and bread. In the next scene, the mean-spirited monopoly capitalist, Mr. Potter, hears one of his aides describe Bailey Park as a collection of "the prettiest little houses you ever saw." Later in the film, of course, the angel Clarence places George Bailey in a world in which he had never been born. Bedford Falls has now become Pottersville, a community of vice, alcoholism, hypocrisy, mental disorder, and dysfunctional families: portent of a suburban nightmare.

Ever since, it seems, these rival images of the American suburb have clashed in our popular culture. The positive view of suburban life took firmest root in the new medium of television. During the late 1950s, this genre found a kind of pop perfection with the Anderson family in *Father Knows Best* (1954-60), the Stone family in *The Donna Reed Show* (1958-66), and the indomitable Cleavers in *Leave it to Beaver* (1957-63). In all of these TV families, we saw professional fathers married to homemaking mothers raising their children to moral maturity in safe, modern suburban communities. Behind the canned laughs, a warm domesticity permeated these fictional homes; the minor crises of the children's lives were invariably resolved in family-strengthening ways.[1]

The dark vision of suburbia came to television somewhat later, first appearing as science fiction. The common theme was the supposed suburban fear of difference. One episode of *The Twilight Zone*, for example, showed paranoid suburbanites tracking down a presumed space alien in their midst. The first true "reality show" on television, the 1973 PBS documentary *An American Family*, placed cameras in and about the Loud family suburban home, expecting to record scenes of familial growth and solidarity. Instead, as the nation watched, the family fell apart, with the son "coming out" as a homosexual and the parents turning to divorce.[2]

Hollywood films cast the suburbs in still darker shades. Stifling suburban conformity and the terror lurking underneath have been common themes. An example is *Poltergeist* (1982), where the domestic calm of the Freeling family is torn apart by ferocious demons, the denizens of an old Indian burial ground under the family's suburban home.

The real fate of the Loud family on television would be replicated in a series of films. Most recently, *American Beauty* (1999)—in one critic's words—"savagely deconstructs the notion of wholesome family values in the heartland of American suburbia."[3]

"Suburbia as Fascism" is another recurrent Hollywood theme. In *The Stepford Wives* (1975), a malevolent husband moves his family from the normalcy of the city out to a suburb where unhappy housewives are transformed into "domesticated and subservient robot replicants."[4] Gary Ross's *Pleasantville* carries this theme to perfection. He shows two contemporary teenagers from a broken home who are magically transported into a 1950s black-and-white television sitcom. As these newcomers expose the TV town to modern art, dirty books, and premarital sex, color appears. As one critic puts it, "*Pleasantville* cleverly satirizes those who preach the virtues of…family values."[5]

The same battle over the meaning of suburbia has taken place in words. Early promoters showed a populist exuberance. Declaring in 1948 that "children and dogs are as necessary to the welfare of this country as is Wall Street and the railroads," President Harry Truman urged passage of a bill to provide "a decent home and suitable living environment for every American family."[6] Bill Levitt, the architect of the famed Levittown developments who was featured on the cover of *Time* magazine in 1950, declared: "For Sale: A New Way of Life." The *Saturday Evening Post* of that era saw the suburban surge "motivated by emotions as strong and deep as those which sent the pioneer wagons rolling westward a century ago."[7] Contemporary historian Michael Johns sees the suburbs of the 1950s as joining together "the classic American forces of cultural assimilation, economic mobility, and ownership of property."[8]

Suburbia's critics were again legion. Lewis Mumford castigated suburban life as "a multitude of uniform houses, lined up inflexibly at uniform distances, on uniform roads…inhabited by people of the same class, the same income, the same age group, witnessing the same television performances, eating the same tasteless pre-fabricated foods."[9] William Whyte, author of *The Organization Man*, stressed how "people's friendships, even their most intimate ones," were predetermined by suburbia's physical layout, denying authentic human bonds.[10] Another critic described the new suburbs as hyper-superficial, "a sorority house with kids." Feminists would condemn this era as "a *foul time* for women and girls."[11] Later critics such as James Howard Kunstler would label "the American automobile utopia known as the suburbs" as "the favorite place of conservative Republicans…their natural habitat…where they spawn and replicate… It is inherently unsuited to be the dwelling place of civilization (or of a restored civic virtue)."[12]

Few suburban critics, though, have surpassed the vitriol of John Keats, author of *The Crack in the Picture Window*:

> Apple Drive, like most developments, is *a jail* of the soul, *a wasteland* of look-alike boxes stuffed with look-alike neighbors. Here there are *no facilities for human life*, other than *bedrooms* and *bathrooms*. Here is a place that lacks the advantages of both city and country but retains the *dis*advantages of each. Each suburban family is somehow a broken home, consisting of a father who appears as an overnight guest, a put-upon housewife with too much to do, and children necessarily brought up in a kind of communism.[13]

My Goodness! Such a nightmare! And yet, positive images of 1950s suburbia haunt our society, to this day. *Leave it to Beaver*, as example, was not a very successful show when it originally aired from 1957 to 1963; it never climbed higher than eighteenth in the Nielsen ratings. Since 1968, though, the show has enjoyed a boisterous syndication, never more so than now. Dozens of *LITB* websites—yes, they have their own moniker—compete today to sell memorabilia. *Beaver* conventions are held. Whole books, written by frenzied academics, have sought to destroy "the Beaver myth": books such as Stephanie Coontz's *The Way We Never Were* and Joanne

Meyerwitz's *Not June Cleaver*, which blasts "the mythic images of cultural icons—June Cleaver, Donna Reed, Harriet Nelson."[14] Stephen Talbot, who as a child actor played the part of Gilbert on *Leave it to Beaver* (his signature line was "Gee, Beav, I don't know"), reported in 1997 that he had spent his entire adult life "trying to conceal my '*Leave it to Beaver*' past.... [T]he series has become inescapable."[15]

Beyond the sad humor, such powerful passions and sharp ideological conflict do suggest that the controversy over images of suburbia may be more important than we usually think. Perhaps it is no coincidence that the most pointed debate between "capitalist" and "communist" during the Cold War was in fact over the meaning of suburban life. The famed "Kitchen Debate," held July 24, 1959, between then U.S. Vice President Richard Nixon and Soviet leader Nikita Khruschev started in a model American suburban home on exhibit in Communist Moscow. Nixon pointed to a built-in control panel for a washing machine, and labeled it "the newest model...the kind which is built in thousands of units for direct installation in [American] houses," to support our homemakers. Khruschev sneered that the Soviets did not have "this capitalist attitude toward women." Nixon retorted: "I think that this attitude toward women is universal. What we want to do is make easier the life of our housewives."[16]

Census 2000 reports that the majority of Americans—over 150 million—now live in suburbs or suburb-like environments. Even in cities, the rise of "urban malls," casual dress, mini-marts, and McDonald's restaurants testifies to the suburbanization of all American life. We are now a suburban people; or, in the title of one recent book, *Suburban Nation*.[17]

On a more immediate note, contemporary scholarly accounts of the suburbs usually point to three nations as classic examples of modern suburban cultures: the United States, Great Britain, and Australia.[18] Is it just a coincidence, again, that these are also the three— indeed, the only three—nations that dispatched combat forces in 2003 to fight in Iraq? Might "suburbia" actually be a concept that embodies not only geography and housing design, but coherent and potent shared values as well? The United Nations failed to act in Iraq. Might future historians characterize the Iraq War as *The Suburban Nations* on the march?

The Suburb as Myth

How then do we sort out the truth about the suburbs, in the 1950s and also today? Let us examine more closely some of the prevailing myths about suburbia.

Myth #1: The suburbs of the 1950s were patriarchal, resting on exaggerated gender differences.

This is surely false, the result of looking backward from today's narrow feminist worldview. Indeed, observers at the time were struck instead by the growing "domestication of the American Male." In 1954, *Life* magazine concluded that, "not since pioneer days, when men built their own log cabins, have they been so personally involved in their homes." In contrast to their fathers, these "new suburban men" constructed backyard patios, entertained business associates in their homes as hosts and bartenders, bought modern time-saving gadgets for the kitchen, tended babies so their wives might go shopping or to club meetings, helped with the marketing, cared for the lawn, and often outnumbered the mothers at school on Parents Day. Even those fathers grilling hamburgers on the backyard barbeque represented a new turn by men to domestic tasks.[19] Suburban man, one study concluded, "can *afford* to orient himself more toward the enjoyment of life in family activities."[20] *McCalls* magazine offered its own explanation, also in 1954:

> Had Ed been a father twenty five years ago, he would have had little time to play and work along with his children. Husbands and fathers were respected then, but they weren't friends and companions to their families. Today, the chores as well as the companionship make Ed part of his family. He and Carol have centered their lives almost completely around their children and their home.[21]

Women, too, were taking on new roles during the supposedly rigid 1950s. A comparison of language in *The Ladies Home Journal* of that decade with language from the 1890-1920 period showed the disappearance of references to femininity and delicacy, replaced in the fifties by a stress on male-female companionship. Similarly, the view of women as subordinate to men completely vanished. (On the other hand, and importantly, there was *no shift* by the 1950s towards more acceptance of working mothers.)[22] A recent scholarly analysis of the ubiquitous Tupperware Party system of the 1950s sees it as a form of "non-radical feminism": "Undermining the postwar image of the housebound, passive, and privatized suburban consumer, Tupperware embodied consumption as a liberating and celebratory form."[23] Indeed, the main worry of psychiatrists in the 1950s was that "the sexes in this country are losing their identity." Patriarchy had vanished; so-called "sexual ambiguity" was the problem.[24]

Myth #2: Suburbia in the 1950s contained a homogeneous population.

It is true that the practice of "red-lining" kept African Americans out of most of the postwar suburbs. And it is also true that the suburbs tended to segregate persons by income, age, and social class: these were *middle-class* creations by new, young families. Yet, in another sense, the postwar suburbs were a *great* experiment in pulling diverse people together. This new generation of white ethnics had left their segregated urban ghettoes—Polish, Italian, Jewish, Swedish, Greek—to coalesce into Americans. This suburbia represented the greatest *mixing* of Protestants, Catholics, and Jews ever recorded in our history. Coming after the challenges of the Great Depression and World War II, this was a period—in Philip Roth's words—of "fierce Americanization," a time of nation-building resting on a common devotion to family creation and "an overall cultural coherence."[25]

Myth #3: The suburbs generated a new wave of mental illness.

Again, not true. In his careful study of one locale, Herbert Gans found "no more mental illness, at least of the kind that surfaces into statistics, in Levittown than in other [suburban] communities, and certainly less than in the cities."[26] Indeed, surveys showed suburbanites to be happy people. Over 80 percent rated their marriages as "above average." Another survey found two out of three labeling their marriage as "extraordinarily happy" or "decidedly happier than average."[27] It's like the so-called Lake Wobegon effect in school testing: all suburban marriages were above average.

Myth #4: The suburbs of the 1950s were highly conformist.

This is probably true. But as Michael Johns correctly asks: "[w]hy would anyone *not* follow the rules, *accept* the codes, and *buy* the entire package of suburban life?" Unlike their parents, the typical suburban couple owned a house in a neighborhood that guarded property values. They enjoyed a rising income and a summer vacation. Their children were healthy, the schools safe. They had confidence in a government that guaranteed mortgages, put veterans through college, built schools and sewer systems, and vaccinated the kids. Moreover, "everyone understood that a cold war was being fought against an enemy whose way of life...was *a threat* to their own."[28] Looking from a different angle, Herbert Gans found so-called suburban "conformity" to represent an "accelerated social life" resting on *more neighboring*, *greater friendliness*, and *enhanced readiness* to provide mutual aid: hardly bad things. The Levittowners made little use of their backyards, focusing instead on the social life of the sidewalks and streets. Rejecting Whyte's claim about the dominant role of propinquity in shaping friendships, Gans found Levittowners choosing instead personally "compatible"—not adjacent—neighbors with whom to socialize.[29]

Myth #5: The suburbs represented the last stand of the traditional family.

This new suburbia was indeed intensely familistic and child-centered. The 1950s embodied a true culture of marriage, where all the signals pointed toward family-building. As one woman put it, the "current of the mainstream was so strong that you only had to step off the bank and float downstream into marriage and motherhood."[30] David Riesman found that young adults "moved to the suburbs for the benefit of the children...for the sake of a better family life."[31] Children were, indeed, everywhere—products of the famous Baby Boom. Female college graduates defied the laws of sociology: their fertility more than doubled. Dennis Brogan reported that "[y]ou can find in people of my [older] generation either wonder and pleasure at the acceptance of the four-child family by their only child, or an irritated bewilderment at such indecently large families."[32]

Yet it is also true that the suburban family was, in a sense, as new as it was traditional.[33] Compared to families in the old ethnic neighborhoods, these homes rested on greater intimacy, companionship, and inward focus. Compared to farm families, the suburban family was a far less functional and a more emotion-driven, child-centered entity. A mere ten percent of suburban mothers with preschool children worked, even part time: well below the figures for city and farm. Compared to both urban and rural family structures, the suburban family was also *more* connected to *voluntary* social, civic and religious groups: Tocquevillians all.

Myth #6: The suburbs created a spiritual vacuum.

In truth, the 1950s witnessed the greatest surge in church membership and church building in American history. Compared to the 1930s, the proportion of the population attending church or synagogue weekly nearly doubled. It is true that many questioned the significance of this. "There has been a revival of religion," Brogan noted, "but that ambiguous term does not imply a revival of the sense of sin." Elting Morison doubted that higher church attendance meant a "daily search for divine guidance" in one's life or building a true personal relationship with God; more likely, he thought, it exhibited growing recognition "of the need for explicit and shared values."[34] Gans said that the Levittowners believed in the value of *church* and *school*, not as transforming institutions, but as places "to support the home and its values."[35] All the same, the new Revised Standard Version of the Bible topped the bestseller list in 1952; indeed, it was the top selling book for the whole decade of the 1950s. A new sense of religiosity spread through American society: "In God We Trust" went on the currency; "under God" into the Pledge of Allegiance.

In short, the suburbs of the 1950s were more complex and more interesting places than the myths would have them be. Herbert Gans is right in chiding most of suburbia's critics as *cosmopolitans* projecting "the alienation they experience in American society onto suburbanites." In attacking the suburbs, they were—in truth—attacking the middle-class, *American* virtues of family, faith, and responsibility.[36] Michael Johns actually sees America reaching its peak—its *Moment of Grace*—as an urban society in this oft-derided decade. It was

> ...the moment when the American city of factories, downtown shopping, and well defined neighborhoods, vitalized by a culture of urbane song, dress, and manners, achieved its consummate expression; when new suburbs relied on cities for jobs and manufactured goods; and when the residents of those suburbs epitomized the nearly dogmatic optimism of the time and belonged to a dense network of groups and associations.[37]

It is important to note, as well, that the suburban boom was also a product of public policy. During the 1930s, the federal government had favored the subsistence homestead of house, garden, and chicken coop on three to five acres. After World War II, suburban developments gained preference and it was federally guaranteed FHA and VA loans that fueled suburbia's spread. Meanwhile, federal funds also built the freeways that bound these new communities to central cities.

Frail Companionship

And yet, this achievement—this "Moment of Grace"—did not last: shortly after 1960, central city and suburb both went into a period of crisis. For suburbia, the cause—at least in part—was the internal weakness of the new suburban family model.

To begin with, this family system rested on the concept of marriage as "companionship in leisure time activities, not on merging every aspect of married life."[38] The new home would be devoted to psychological intimacy, love, and democracy, with the family resting on "the mutual affection, the sympathetic understanding, and the comradeship of its members."[39]

This also meant accepting the home-without-material-function as a positive good. For the prior hundred years, the family had been shedding its historic functions: the making of clothes, the processing of food, and the crafting of soap, candles, and other commodities went to the factories; education and child protection went to governments. The suburban home would *complete this abdication of useful tasks*. Architects concluded that housing "inherited from the family farm" should be replaced by modern, flexible designs. "The goal of home construction" would be "a frictionless family life." Sheds, storage cellars, attics, workrooms, loom and sewing rooms, parlors, and large kitchens must all go. The "companionship family," the Federal Housing Administration concluded, needed "space and facilities for nurturing," not for work: it wanted ambiguous spaces such as "the family room." The great divorce of home and workplace must be made final, and complete.[40] Accordingly, government backed mortgages would be denied to any residence that contained space for an office, productive shop, separate apartment, or small business. Lawns would be allowed, and encouraged. But large vegetable gardens were questionable. Modest animal husbandry, such as a rabbit hutch or chicken coop, forbidden.

There were other fragile aspects to the suburban family. Herbert Gans shows that suburbs like Levittown were built with small children in mind, and that most children were satisfied there. But he also acknowledges that adolescents had no respectable and nearby place to go, "nothing to do." The bedrooms were too small for adolescent use; the shopping malls too far away; there were few low-rent shopping areas that could survive on the marginal purchases of adolescents.[41] Moreover, although women were generally happy in suburbia, there was a minority who reported "boredom" and "loneliness," the result of the husband's absence during the day and separation from extended kin.[42]

Indeed, the suburbs were also too modern, too bound up with a complete break from the past. Fashion dictated that the modern living room not be cluttered up by old furniture and other family heirlooms. Meanwhile, the faith in progress and boundless optimism of the suburbanites also led to a curious disrespect for nature and the broader environment.

And then, the suburbs began to change. Some of these alterations were benign, or even positive, relative to the family. The age segregation found in the postwar era inevitably gave way to a greater mixing of the generations. Fair housing laws opened the suburbs to minorities, as well. Offices, distribution centers, and even factories left the downtowns, settling in the suburban "edge cities." The classic commute from suburb to downtown was frequently replaced by the suburb-to-suburb drive.

Other changes, however, reflected a diminished commitment to family life. Between 1960 and 1977, marital fertility in America fell 40 percent, a change concentrated in the suburbs. And while divorce remained less common there than in the cities, it nonetheless climbed.[43] Federally guaranteed mortgages, once funneled by law and custom overwhelmingly toward young, newly married couples, were partially redirected, to the benefit of divorced and never-married householders.[44]

Home architecture changed, as well. Suburbs of the 1950s were front yard and sidewalk oriented; by the 1980s, sidewalks had disappeared, huge three-car garages dominated the front yards, and household life reoriented toward the back. In new suburbs such as Naperville, Illinois, one analyst noted, "it seems much more possible [now] not to know your neighbors." Inside homes, the living and dining rooms were shrinking, becoming "vestigial spaces" alongside the front hall and reflecting a retreat from home entertainment. Meanwhile, *master bedrooms* swelled in size while *bathrooms* increased in number and luxury: by the 1990s, one bath per bedroom was the construction norm.[45] John Keat's snobbish sneer in 1960 toward the suburb—"Here there are no facilities for human life other than bedrooms and bathrooms"—actually seemed to be coming true.

The largest change—indeed the one driving most of the others—was the rapid emergence of the suburban working mother. Where only 10 percent of suburban mothers of preschoolers worked in 1960, about 75 percent did by 1990, part- and full-time. Changes in policy (Title VII of the Civil Rights Act of 1964), in ideology (the new feminism), in culture (the diminished status of homemaking), and in economics (market adjustments to a two income norm) lay behind this development. For suburban neighborhoods, this meant a great emptying during the daylight hours: fathers to their workplace, just as before; mothers now to their workplaces as well; and the children to the daycare center, the all-day kindergarten, or the school and after-school program. The suburban home and way-of-life had been designed around the fulltime mother and homemaker: she was the *linchpin* of the system, the *nucleus* of the suburban nuclear family. With her gone, an eerie silence ensued over the expensive daylight ghost towns of late twentieth-century suburbia. The nights, in Nicholas Lemann's words, meant being "stressed out in suburbia."[46]

Working mothers, of course, had less time and inclination toward children: one perhaps; sometimes two. As the number of bedrooms rose in the average suburban home, the number of children shrank, and even those left reported a new sense of disorder. In his comprehensive study of American youth, Francis Ianni found many suburban adolescents confused by their "early emancipation" from family life, due to mother's employment and—sometimes—divorce. These youth complained that "there was nothing to do and frequently expressed resentment at being abandoned by parents." The researcher voiced concern about these "sullen and often disruptive bands of youngsters involuntarily liberated from parental guidance and supervision.... To some extent, these peer groups are the suburban equivalents of the urban street gangs."[47]

Curiously, the *diminished* nature of suburban family life even accounts for the newest charge leveled against the suburbs: "suburban sprawl." Anti-sprawl activists denounce the overzealous development of new subdivisions and malls, and blame it on over population, the dreaded result of suburban fertility. In fact, the real problem is almost the reverse. It is true that the overall American population grew from 179 million in 1960 to 281 million in 2000, an increase of 57 percent. Yet the number of households, *requiring separate shelter*, grew by *100* percent, from 52.8 million in 1960 to 105 million in 2000. Why the discrepancy? Simply put: the retreat from family living. In 1960, 75 percent of all American households were "married couple households" and average household size was 3.4 persons. By 2000, though, married couples comprised only about 50 percent of households and average household size had fallen to 2.5. All the growth was in the never-married, divorced, and "childless cohabiting" categories. Indeed, if the suburban family model of 1960 could be magically imposed on the American populace of 2003, the USA would actually need 28 million *fewer* dwelling units than it now has. Put another way, *marriage* and *larger* families actually prove to be *more environment-friendly* than singles and childless couples. Why? Larger families—on a *per capita basis*—*use less* land, building materials, fuel, food, and supplies; they are more efficient. In January 2003, the leading environmental journal *Nature* calculated that if the projected average household size of developed nations for 2015 was the same as it had been in 1985, *415 million fewer housing units* would be needed worldwide. Again, *family breakdown*, not too many people, seems to be the primary cause of modern *suburban sprawl*.[48]

Ideas for Renewal

The key question follows: Can the suburbs be renewed as vital centers for family living? I believe they can, but only if we consciously guide them toward healing the great divorce between home and work, bringing *both* parents back in the home for child-centered ends.

This is why the so-called New Urbanism is a step in the right direction, but *only* a step. This movement among architects and urban planners calls for more diverse neighborhoods designed to accommodate pedestrians as well as autos. The return of sidewalks, small front lots, large front porches, and garages on alleys are parts of their scheme. Well-defined and easily accessible community centers and public spaces, they argue, should also guide suburban design. Small shopping districts should be in walking distance, and cater to the needs of adults, children, and adolescents; the latter, in particular, should have "honorable gathering places." Architecture and landscaping should boisterously incorporate local history and building practices and show ecological sensitivity.[49]

These are all worthy ideas, but they remain incomplete. They aim at renewed "community," understood as block, neighborhood, and polis. But the New Urbanists say little about families, except to note, accept, and even praise their new diversity. This probably reflects the origin of the New Urbanism on the cultural and environmental left, where "family values" in any traditional sense hold little sway.

For twenty-first-century families, the deeper need is *refunctionalized homes*. Family life will broadly thrive again, whether in "old" suburbs or "new urbanist" ones, only when both parents are relodged in homes that are *beehives* of daily activity. "Productive homes," not "companionate homes," are the imperative need. *Only this* will start to heal the breach between work and home caused by the urban-industrial revolution, a divide that the "gawky" but "healthy and happy" suburbs of the 1950s were decidedly unable to bridge.

In practice, what would this mean? Some of the specifics are already clear:

* *We can see home schools*, where families are reclaiming the vital education function from the state and regrounding parents (mostly mothers at this point) and children in their homes and neighborhoods;
* *and we can see the "wired" home*, where the web and the modern computer make it possible to renew the family home as a place of commerce and the professions.

And yet, government regulations still maintain large barriers to the progress of this broad pro-family revolution. FHA underwriting rules sharply restrict the kinds of work that can be done in homes. Zoning laws, a relatively recent product from the 1920s, remain implicitly tied to the weak "companionship model" of family life. In most places, it is nearly impossible to operate a business (with visiting customers) or a preschool or a professional office out of one's home.

Even worse, it turns out, are the Neighborhood or Homeowner Associations, a new kind of informal governance that has recorded rapid growth at the same time as suburban family life has declined. A product of the 1960s, Homeowner Associations now embrace 50 million Americans. Using restrictive covenants and liens-on-homes to enforce their wills, these Associations are—in analyst Spencer MacCallum's words—far more "arbitrary, unresponsive, and dictatorial" than zoning boards in their control over the lives of residents. Commonly prohibiting everything from home offices to swing sets and picket fences, Homeowner Associations—in one critic's words— provide neither liberty, nor justice, nor domestic tranquility.[50]

The iron grip of state boards governing the professions of law, accounting, medicine, dentistry, and so on also limit the prospects for family renewal. Once practiced out of homes, these professions reorganized on industrial models in the twentieth century: massive professional schools have replaced apprenticeships just as mass clinics have displaced the office-in-the-home, changes aided and abetted by state regulation. With modest exceptions, modern technologies of learning, communication, research, and practice no longer make this necessary.

What is the solution? In one word: Liberty. We need to tear back the web of regulations that prevent families from being full, rich, and productive. Specifically:

- At the federal level, we should abolish FHA and other public underwriting rules that limit the creation of home offices, home schools, and home businesses.
- At the state level, we should abolish those regulations of the professions—medicine, law, dentistry, accounting, and so on—which favor giant institutions and prohibit decentralized learning such as apprenticeships; standardized exams alone should determine competence and licensing.
- At the local level, zoning laws should be loosened or even abolished, to allow the flourishing of home gardens, modest animal husbandry, home offices and businesses, and home schools. In place of zoning, the more flexible "nuisance laws" of the early twentieth century should be restored as guardians of neighborhood tranquility.
- At the neighborhood or "development" level, "restrictive covenants" that bind families to the failed "companionship" lifestyle should be loosened, if possible; Homeowner Associations in new developments should be discouraged.
- And at the cultural level, we should look to the creation of intentional family-centered communities by religious peoples. Co-believers might create towns and communities built around worship, mutual obligation, and the rearing of children, living environments that could encourage the productive home *and* spiritual vitality.[51]

From this new birth of freedom, we can even imagine the lonely contemporary American suburbs reborn, with small shops where ghostly living rooms once stood; with lawyers, doctors, and dentists again working out of home offices, assisted by able young apprentices; with productive gardens and modest animal life; and with the midday laughter of home-schooled children where only silence had prevailed. This is an environment where the great breach between home and work might heal, and where marriage and the child-rich family, embedded in real community, might flourish again in this, "The Suburban Century."

Notes

1.   On this genre, see: Lynn Spigel, "From Theatre to Space Ship: Metaphors of Suburban Domesticity in Postwar America," in Roger Silverstone, ed., *Visions of Suburbia* (London and New York: Routledge, 1997): 221-24.

2.   Spigel, "From Theatre to Spaceship," pp. 224, 232.

3.   Greg King, "American Beauty," at http://www.all-reviews.com/videos/americanbeauty-10.htm.

4.   Spigel, "From Theatre to Space Ship," p. 227.

5.   Schlomo Schwartzberg, "*Pleasantville*," at http://www.boxoff.com.

6.   "Housing Gets No. 1 Spot at Family Life Conference," *Journal of Housing* (May 1948): 15.

7.   Harold Martin, "Are We Building a City 600 Miles Long?" *Saturday Evening Post* (Jan. 2, 1960).

8.   Michael Johns, *Moment of Grace: The American City in the 1950s* (Berkeley: University of California Press, 2003): 94.

9.   Lewis Mumford, *The City in History* (New York: Harcourt Brace, 1961): 486.

10. William H. Whyte, Jr., "How the New Suburbia Socializes," *Fortune* 48 (Aug. 1953): 120-22.

11. Michele Landsberg, "'Family Values' a Myth of Suburban 1950s," *The Toronto Star* (Dec. 10, 2000).

12. James Howard Kunstler, "A Virtual Public Realm is not Good Enough," *The American Enterprise* (Fall 1997); at http://www.kunstler.com/mags_am_ent.html.

13. John Keats, "Compulsive Suburbia," *The Atlantic Monthly* 205 (April 1960): 47-50.

14. Stephanie Coontz, *The Way We Never Were* (New York: Basic Books, 1992); and Joanne Meyerowitz, *Not June Cleaver* (Philadelphia: Temple University Press, 1994).

15. Stephen Talbot, "Living Down Beaver," at http://www.salon.com/aug97/mothers/beaver970822.html.

16. CNN Interactive, "Cold War; Episode 14: Red Spring," at http://www.cnn.com/specials/cold.war/episodes/14/documents/debate/.

17. Andres Duany, Elizabeth Plater-Zyberk, and Jeff Speck, *Suburban Nation* (New York: North Point Press, 2001).

18. A point made most recently in: Silverstone, *Visions of Suburbia*, p. 4.

19. "The New American Domesticated Male: A Boon to the Household and a Boom for Industry," *Life* 36 (Jan. 4, 1954): 42-45; "The Weekend Woe of a Father Named Joe: He Gives the Wife Time Off and Bravely Takes Charge," *Life* 41 (July 16, 1956): 85-89; and "Outdoor Cooking: Barbecue Boom Smokes Up U.S.," *Life* 35 (July 20, 1953): 49.

20. Robert O. Blood, Jr. and Donald M. Wolfe, *Husbands and Wives: The Dynamics of Married Life* (Glencoe, IL: The Free Press of Glencoe, 1960): 61.

21. Quotation from: Johns, *Moment of Grace*, p. 101.

22.   Sanford M. Dornbusch and Caroline Roberts, "Perception of Women in the Ladies Home Journal, 1890-1955," Unpublished paper, 1957.
23.   Alison J. Clarke, "Tupperware: Suburbia, Sociality, and Mass Consumption," in Silverstone, *Visions of Suburbia*, pp. 134-56.
24.   From *Life* (Dec. 24, 1956); quoted in Clyde Kluckhohn, "Have There Been Discernible Shifts in American Values During the Past Generation?" in Elting E. Morison, ed., *The American Style: Essays in Value and Performance* (New York: Harper and Brothers, 1958): 201.
25.   See: Johns, *Moment of Grace*, p. 5.
26.   Herbert Gans, *The Levittowners: Ways of Life and Politics in a New Suburban Community* (New York: Pantheon Books, 1967): 236.
27.   In Johns, *Moment of Grace*, p. 114.
28.   Ibid.
29.   Gans, *The Levittowners*, pp. 157-59.
30.   Brett Harvey, *The Fifties: A Woman's Oral History* (New York: Harper-Collins, 1993): xiii.
31.   David Riesman, "The Found Generation," *The American Scholar* (Autumn 1956).
32.   Dennis W. Brogan, "Unnoticed Changes in America." *Harpers* (Feb. 1957).
33.   Johns, *Moment of Grace*, p. 95.
34.   Kluckhohn, "Shifts in Values During the Past Generation," p. 180.
35.   Gans, *The Levittowners*, p. 28.
36.   Ibid., pp. 234, 240.
37.   Johns, *Moment of Grace*, p. 1.
38.   Blood and Wolfe, *Husbands and Wives*, p. 173.
39.   Ernest W. Burgess and Henry V. Locke, *The Family* (New York: American Book Company, 1945): 654-72.
40.   See: John P. Dean, "Housing Design and Family Values," *Land Economics* 29 (May 1953): 128-41; Svend Reimer, "Architecture for Family Living," *Journal of Social Issues* 7 (1951): 140-51; and Gertrude Sipperly Fish, ed., *The Story of Housing* (New York: Macmillan, 1979): 476-78.
41.   Gans, *The Levittowners*, pp. 206-09.
42.   Ibid., pp. 231-33.
43.   According to a 1982 survey, among women whose first marriages had survived at least ten years, 44 percent of those in central cities saw them terminated during the next 15 years, compared to 21 percent in the suburbs. See: Luiza W. Chan and Tim B. Heaton, "Demographic Determinants of Delayed Divorce," *Journal of Divorce* 13 (1987): 97-103.
44.   See: Allan C. Carlson, *From Cottage to Work Station* (San Francisco: Ignatius Press, 1993): 80-82.
45.   Nicholas Lemann, "Stressed Out in Suburbia," *The Atlantic* 264 (Nov. 1989): 42-43.
46.   Lemann, "Stressed Out in Suburbia," p. 40.
47.   Francis A. J. Ianni, *The Search for Structure: A Report on American Youth Today* (New York: The Free Press, 1989): 84-85, 206-07.
48.   Jiangu Liu, Gretchen C. Dally. Paul E. Ehrlich, and Gary W. Luck, "Effects of Household Dynamics on Resource Consumption and Biodiversity," *Nature* 421 (Jan. 30, 2003): 530-33.
49.   Kunstler, "A Virtual Public Realm is not Good Enough," p. 2; Michael Leccese and Kathleen McCormick, eds., *Charter of the New Urbanism* (New York: McGraw-Hill, 1999); and Peter Katz and Vincent Scully, Jr., *The New Urbanism: Toward an Architecture of Community* (New York, NY: McGraw-Hill, 1993).

50.   See: Spencer Heath MacCallum, "The Case for Land Lease Versus Subdivision: Homeowners' Associations Reconsidered," in David T. Beito, Peter Gordon, and Alexander Tabarrok, eds., *The Voluntary City* (Ann Arbor: University of Michigan Press, 2002): 371-79.
51.   One architect giving this idea attention is Philip Bess of the firm Thursday Architects in Chicago (http://thursdayarchitects.com). See: Philip Bess, "Making Sacred: The Phenomenology of Matter and Spirit in Architecture and the City," *Civitas* 3 (1996): and Philip Bess, "Virtuous Reality: Critical Realism and the Reconstruction of Architectural and Urban Theory," *The Classicist* 3 (1996).

6

Taxing the Family: An American Version of Paradise Lost?

With a surprisingly regularity, the tax reform issue has returned to challenge the 108th Congress, just as it has appeared every second year since 1995. The Washington army of "special interests" has gathered again, with each constituency group ready to protect its favored portions of the U.S. Tax Code and to leverage its share of any new reform.

Joining the joint-stock corporations, trade associations, labor unions, and charities in the jockeying this time have been lifestyle advocates with distinctive visions of fairness. Equity feminists, for example, yearn to replace the "joint return" for married couples with mandatory individual filing, to eliminate "marriage" as a tax category, and to shift the tax burden onto "homemakers" and one-income families.[1] Homosexual advocates, for their part, seek to end the "privileging" of heterosexuality in the tax code and "the non-marriage penalty imposed on those who cannot marry."[2]

As these examples suggest, judgments regarding the nature of social life have become deeply entwined with the existing U.S. Tax Code. Congress can no longer be counted on to protect the interests of American homes by its group instinct alone; perhaps it never could. In any case, advocates for the traditional family have a special need at this time to understand both the history and current status of family relations relative to federal taxation. Specifically: What ideological forces have shaped contemporary tax policy? What past or existing tax policies have been clearly family-friendly? What policies have been hostile? What priorities should family advocates adopt in 2004?

Any judgment on taxation of the home must rest on a clear definition of the healthy family. For the purposes of this chapter, tax policy will be considered "good" if it protects or favors marriage, marital fertility, and the economic integrity of the home. It will be considered "hostile" if it penalizes or discourages the marital bond, the birth of children, and the home economy. What is the rationale for these principles?

First, the marriage of a man and a woman is more than another lifestyle choice. It marks the founding of a new home, a new "cell" of society, and forms the biological conditions for the creation of new human life and the rearing of these children in a responsible setting. The social gifts of marriage are vast. Children growing up with their married natural parents are—when compared to *all* other possible arrangements—much *less* likely to be sexually, physically, or mentally abused,[3] to attempt suicide,[4] to abuse alcohol or take illegal drugs,[5] and to commit delinquent or criminal acts.[6] Married parents are healthier, in mind and body, than their never-married or divorced counterparts.[7] The children of the married are also more likely to be healthy and happy and to do well in school than children reared in any other setting.[8] These gifts result in stronger communities, a more engaged citizenry, higher government revenues, and lower government expenses.

As a corollary, divorce should be discouraged. Except in cases of physical abuse between husband and wife, divorce has a strong negative effect on children. All measures of child well being show, on average, negative turns following the divorce decree.[9] Among the former spouses, moreover, gauges of physical and mental health also deteriorate after divorce, underscoring the broad social costs of breaking apart the home.[10]

Second, the birth and nurture of children is the central purpose of society. Married parents who commit to the rearing of children are doing more than making a consumption choice. They are assuming sacrifices and taking on responsibilities that are vitally necessary for the future of society. Accordingly, tax policy should protect and favor married parenthood and children. Tax preferences for dependent offspring are also the least intrusive way to compensate households for the clear "market failure" regarding children. Competitive wage markets simply do not pay attention to the number of dependents a worker might have. Social democratic nations usually turn to state child allowances as a response. However, these payments tend to draw governments deeply into the family economy and to substitute state largesse for parental earnings. Universal and child-

sensitive tax exemptions, deductions, and credits, in contrast, require no intrusion by the state into the family, beyond proof of a
child's birth. These tax measures allow the family to *keep more of
what it earns* while the young are in the home. Children still properly see their parents, rather than the state, as their providers. Moreover, in an era of zero- or negative-long-term fertility among the
developed nations, the birth of additional children can be seen as a
positive good and a stimulus to economic expansion.[11]

*Finally, the strength of the home rests on the resilience of the home
economy.* The family household operates on the principles of love,
sharing, and altruism. It provides food, clothing, shelter, and care to
the young, the old, the sick, and the infirm: those who cannot provide for themselves. The strong home represents, as well, an economic exchange between husband and wife resting on the specialization of their labor and the pooling of income and expenses. These
exchanges, usually occurring on a non-cash basis, are the lifeblood
of the home. Accordingly, they should be free of all taxation, direct
or indirect.

Experience also shows that federal tax policy can have a marked
effect on the level of individual commitment to the household
economy. For example, mandatory individual taxation of all adults
sharply reduces the commitment of women and men to home-based
child and elder care and other forms of home production.[12] Con-
versely, one consequence of high marginal tax rates in a regime of
joint returns for the married is to encourage more home production
and less time in the marketplace.[13] From the perspective of the family, then, wise and just tax policy defends the boundary between the
market economy and the home economy, keeping the latter free of
state intrusion and extraction.

Based on these principles, how has the federal tax system treated
the family since the introduction of the income tax in 1913?

For the first thirty years, the federal record was fairly dismal. Some
influential figures, such as former president Theodore Roosevelt,
urged generous tax deductions favoring marriage and children.[14]
However, the Revenue Acts of 1913 and 1916 were instead highly
individualistic. Congress made the individual, rather than the family
household, the taxable entity. Married couples could file joint returns under the 1916 Act, but gained no real advantage in doing so.
Dependent exemptions were allowed during the 1916-1943 period,
but they had no necessary relationship to family bonds. In short, the

federal income tax basically ignored the family, in favor of efficiency, progressivity, and individualism.[15]

Trends in family life during this period were also negative. The birth rate declined by a third between 1913 and 1940, while the divorce rate rose and the proportion of the adult population who were married fell. Prominent sociologists focused on the family's "loss of function" and institutional decline, concluding that "there is a considerable and increasing disorganization of the family."[16] There is some evidence, moreover, that these trends were a partial consequence of the negative tax treatment of the family.[17]

However, a serendipitous force pushing for policy change was a 1930 U.S. Supreme Court decision (*Poe v. Seaborn*), which held that in so-called "community property" states, income splitting for married couples must be permitted. This allowed married couples to file a joint return, where they added up their total income and "split" that sum down the middle, with each spouse effectively taxed on his or her half alone. Under progressive rates (and except for those rare cases where husband and wife each earned exactly the same amount of market income), this measure gave a real benefit to marriage, and to specialization within marriage. While confined in 1930 to those Southwestern states under the residual influence of Spanish law, the community property system began spreading to other states, as legislators responded to married couples seeking to enjoy the marriage-centered tax cut implicit to income splitting. When the U.S. House of Representatives Ways and Means Committee sought in 1941 to alter the law so that *all* married couples would pay the same tax on their consolidated income as a single person with the same amount of income, the idea was beaten back as "a tax on morality" and an incentive to divorce.[18]

Instead, the U.S. Congress began to move in a very different direction. The Reform Act of 1944 created the uniform per capita exemption. In prior decades, personal exemptions had varied widely depending on one's status. In 1925, for example, a married couple received a $3,500 exemption, a single person $1,500, and each dependent $400. For reasons partly of simplicity in administration, Congress adopted a uniform $500 per person exemption in 1944 for the wartime income surtax, and extended it to normal taxation in 1946.

Another purpose, though, was pro-family in intent. These years saw a broad surge of interest in preservation and protection of the family. The social programs of the late New Deal, for example, aimed specifically at creating a "family wage" for fathers in order to support a "mother at home" for the sake of the children. Most recently, the Social Security Amendments of 1939—with strong bipartisan support—had sharply altered the new American welfare system, giving retirement benefits to homemakers and survivor benefits to children. As the key Democratic activist Molly Dewson explained in 1940:

> When you begin to help the family to attain some security you are at the same time beginning to erect a National Structure for the same purpose. Through the well-being of the family, we create the well-being of the Nation. Through our constructive contributions to the one, we help the other to flourish.[19]

These sentiments, reinforced by the pathos of wartime, spread to tax policy as well. As a Ways and Means Committee Report explained, the 1944 Act creating a uniform exemption should impose a "lesser burden on the taxpayers with a large family and a greater burden on taxpayers with a smaller family."[20] Moreover, for the first time, the Act limited the personal exemption only to those household members related by the clear family criteria of "blood, marriage, or adoption."

In 1948, a Republican Congress—over President Harry Truman's veto—forced through a new tax reform measure. With the Treasury running a surplus that year of $8.4 billion, the primary goal was to cut taxes, and Congress did so in a family-supportive way. Forty percent of the tax cut was achieved by raising the personal exemption by one fifth, to $600 per person, or about 18 percent of median household income. This meant that a married couple with three children, earning the median national income of $3,000, would be relieved of any income tax by this provision alone. Another 13 percent of the tax cut came through the universal introduction of income splitting, extending to all forty-eight states the incentive to marriage and the penalties on divorce implicit to this measure.[21]

The 1948 Act also expanded the generous treatment accorded owner-occupied housing: the "imputed rent" of the home was exempted from taxation; the interest on mortgages was also exempted, as were most capital gains from the sale of a house if a new one was purchased within a given time. Veterans Administration (VA) and Federal Housing Administration (FHA) regulations, in conjunction with underwriters' guidelines, delivered over 98 percent of these new, tax-favored mortgages to young married couples.[22] Since a wife's market earnings were not counted when lenders calculated a family's eligibility for a mortgage, the incentives restrained the cost of housing and further encouraged young mothers to become home-makers, with their focus on home production. Econometric analysis showed that about 25 percent of the growth in homeownership in the 1945-75 period was a direct consequence of the tax system's favorable treatment of owner-occupied family housing.[23]

Accordingly, by 1948, the United States could claim a powerfully pro-family tax code, focused on the "breadwinner-homemaker" model:

(1) The progressivity of tax tables was sharply reduced in a manner that favored marriage and children, with the presence of a spouse and off-spring serving as the average household's most important tax shelters;

(2) there was a strong financial incentive for adults to marry and a signifi-cant, indirect penalty for divorce;

(3) the costs of childrearing were fairly recognized; indeed, the per capita exemption actually provided a special bonus for truly large families;

(4) as the tax code worked in conjunction with other government pro-grams, family housing enjoyed a dramatic boom; and

(5) commitment to the household economy was encouraged by high mar-ginal tax rates in conjunction with income splitting.

Over the following fifteen years, the United States enjoyed both unprecedented economic expansion and remarkable social health. Marriages were more stable than in prior decades, and the propor-tion of adults who were married reached an historic high. Following a postwar "spike" in 1946, the divorce rate steadily declined. The "baby boom" also roared into high gear, with marital fertility nearly doubling between 1944 and 1957. Indeed, demographer Leslie Whittington has shown a "robust" relationship between fertility and the real, after-inflation value of the personal income tax exemption, calculating an elasticity of birth probability with respect to the ex-emption of between .839 and 1.31. The Baby Boom of the 1950s, she implies, was in significant degree the consequence of positive tax reform.[24] Policy, it appeared, had been translated into family strength.

Almost from the beginning, though, critics assailed the 1948 re-forms. Income splitting drew the loudest complaints. One concern came from widows and other non-married persons with family de-pendents. Congress responded in 1951 by extending some of the benefits of income splitting to these categories of taxpayers, under the category "head of household."[25] While this seemed reasonable at the time, the change would develop into a modest incentive for divorce and childrearing outside of marriage.[26] Other complaints revealed a deep hostility to the very essence of the 1948 tax regime. One influential analyst claimed to see no virtue in a system that gave a benefit to a person just because he or she had acquired a spouse, rather than spending money in other ways.[27] Another argued that "[a]t the top of the income scale, the major rationale of income taxation is to cut down on the economic power of the family unit," a goal compromised by the 1948 reforms.[28] Economist Michael J. Boskin complained that income splitting "produces a dead weight loss to society," particularly as it induced "a larger decline in the market work of wives relative to husbands than is socially optimal."[29]

By the late 1950s, moreover, a growing segment of elite opinion came to worry about "overpopulation" in America. Advocates of population control indicted the favorable tax treatment given to children as one cause of America's dreaded "three-child family system."[30] Paul Ehrlich, author of the influential volume *The Population Bomb*, called for tax reforms that would reverse the incentives, penalizing all families with children, but especially those "irresponsible" couples with more than two.[31] President Richard Nixon's Commission on Population Growth and The American Future set out to "neutralize...those legal, social and institutional pressures that historically have been mainly pro-natalist in character," including tax benefits keyed to family size.[32]

This new "anti-natalist" mood helps account for the most significant shift in tax law affecting families after 1960. This was the largely invisible erosion in the value of the personal exemption, both in terms of inflation and as an offset against average household income. Congressional population control advocates welcomed this decay as a quiet way to reign in the Baby Boom. According to one analyst writing in 1983, this change would become "[b]y almost any measure...the largest single change in the income tax in the postwar era."[33]

A more direct dismantling of the pro-family tax code won in 1948 also began in the mid-1960s. President John F. Kennedy's celebrated 1963 tax cut, for example, did not raise the value of the personal exemption, as it should have done if the principles of 1948 had been followed. Rather, the measure created a new "standard deduction" that paid no attention to the presence of children, focusing instead on relief for taxpayers with the smallest incomes.[34] This measure also introduced the first of soon-to-be-many "marriage penalties," since the new deduction for a married couple was less than twice as large as that enjoyed by singles.

Later in that decade, complaints that "singles" were treated unfairly under income splitting reached the ear of Representative Wilbur Mills, powerful chairman of the House Ways and Means Committee. In 1969, he expressed interest in extending tax relief to help "bachelors and spinsters as well as widows and widowers," while retaining the "marriage incentive" for those under age thirty-five. Notably, he chose this age level to encourage marriage among younger, more fertile adults. The House-approved bill carried this distinction. Yet the new Nixon administration's tax reform proposal eliminated the age restriction altogether, deeming it "arbitrary."[35] Instead, it proposed limiting the gains to married couples from income splitting to 20 percent of total tax. It was this universalized measure that won adoption in the Tax Reform Act of 1969. Not only did this abandonment of true income splitting sharply reduce the "marriage incentive," it also created another "marriage penalty," which affected some two-income couples with particular force. It created a situation where they would, in fact, be better off single rather than married.

The 1970s were witness to a mounting critique of the favorable tax treatment accorded the "household economy." Some critics saw even residual income splitting as giving too much benefit to families with a mother-at-home. As June O'Neill of the Urban Institute explained, "a system of joint filing is likely to discourage the market employment of married women."[36] "Two job couples" became the newest "Victims of Tax Injustice" demanding compensation for their loss of home production.[37] Other critics said that it was unfair to leave "home production" untaxed, since this encouraged people to produce their own goods and services instead of buying them, which diminished the revenue base.[38] But since it was difficult to measure, and hence tax, home production, policy architects recommended instead that targeted tax cuts be given to households with working wives, which would have the same, albeit indirect effect.

Accordingly, in 1972, Congress increased the value and availability of the tax deduction for non-parental childcare. Four years later, it substituted the Dependent Care Tax Credit, which granted direct tax relief of up to $800 to working parents who put their small children in institutional care. Similarly, Congress' attempt to reduce the "marriage penalty" in 1981 tax legislation (by permitting a partial deduction on the second income of a two-earner household) also enjoyed the same expert rationale: this was a way to "balance" or indirectly tax the extra "imputed income" produced by the home labor within the "one job" household. As intended, these measures encouraged an accelerated flow of mothers into the job market.

At the same time, the housing provisions of the income tax code ceased to have a pro-family effect. FHA and VA eligibility standards were loosened, with the consequence being the funneling of substantially more loans to non-family households.[39] Indeed, by the early 1980s, some housing analysts suspected that a truly unusual, even perverse process had emerged. As economists George Sternlieb and James Hughes explained: "The very decline in the size of household, with its nominal generation of increased demand for housing units, may in turn be a consequence of the availability and costs of housing units generally."[40] Put another way, the tax-favored housing system had now developed a vested interest in divorce and family disruption, where housing supply pushed artificial demand, and where federal housing subsidies—including tax benefits—now served as a substitute for the economic gains once provided by marriage and as a stimulus to divorce.

Meanwhile, mounting inflation accelerated the erosion of the personal exemption. Even its increase from $600 to $1,000 in 1969 did little to help. Together with the changes cited above, families with children became the big losers in the income tax sweepstakes. Between 1948 and 1984, single persons and married couples without children showed no real increase in their average net federal tax rate. In contrast, married couples with two children saw their average net income tax rate rise by 43 percent (from 6.9 to 9.9 percent), while a couple with four children faced a dramatic 223 percent increase (from 2.6 to 8.4 percent).[41]

Another development in this period was the creation of the Earned Income Tax Credit [EITC] in 1975, a modest income supplement made available to low-income households with at least one dependent child at home. It is important to remember that the EITC was conceived as a tax rebate to the working poor with children: its maximum benefit level was initially keyed to the combined total payroll tax rate (both employers and employees portions). With pro-work *and* pro-child credentials, the measure quickly became popular on both sides of the political aisle. Unfortunately, repeated increases in its value soon strained the measure's positive impact and created still another "marriage penalty."

In short, the 1963-85 period were years of loss for the family, relative to federal taxation. Conscious policy changes, in league with inflation, had these consequences:

(1)   Families raising dependent children faced ever heavier federal taxes, both absolutely, and in comparison to single persons and childless couples; and the larger the family, the greater the increased burden;

(2)   "income splitting" disappeared as a guiding concept, reducing the incentive to marriage, creating a disincentive in its place, and generating a modest reward for divorce;

(3)   indirect taxation of the "household economy" appeared for the first time under the guise of the Dependent Care Tax Credit, followed by the 1981 "correction" to the existing "marriage penalty"; and

(4)   tax incentives to owner-occupied housing ceased to have a pro-family effect; indeed, there was mounting evidence that these incentives (in conjunction with other policy shifts) now damaged the interests of families, and even encouraged family breakup.

There can be little doubt that these shifts in the tax treatment of families had something to do with the negative turns in family life that began in the mid-1960s. The number of divorces climbed from 393,000 in 1960 to 1,213,000 in 1981, with the divorce rate rising 140 percent. The rate of first marriage fell 30 percent in the same period. Among women aged twenty to twenty-four, the decline was a stunning 59 percent. The U.S. fertility rate tumbled from 118 (per 1000 women aged fifteen to forty-four) in 1960 to 65.6 in 1978. The number of legal abortions climbed from 745,000 in 1973 to 1,577,000 in 1981. The U.S. total fertility rate, which measures the ability of this society to reproduce, fell into the negative column for the first time in 1971, remaining there into the 1980s.

Then came the sweeping Tax Reform Act of 1986. The pro-family movement represented by groups such as The Family Research Council, it is true, was taking form at this time and starting to give attention to tax policy. It was in 1986, for example, that President Ronald Reagan's White House Working Group on the Family, chaired by Education Undersecretary Gary Bauer, recommended an increase in the per capita value of the personal exemption for children to $5,000.[42] However, the tax reform push in 1986 would largely be guided by other, more libertarian principles. Indeed, partly as a consequence of its reluctance to give first consideration to families, Congress turned to a radically different approach. Its features included:

- the reduction of multiple tax brackets—ranging from 11 to 50 percent on regular income—to only two: 15 percent and 28 percent;
- an increase in the personal exemption to $2,000 by 1989, and its indexing thereafter to inflation; however, personal exemptions would now be phased out for higher income households (above $71,900 for joint returns, and $43,150 for singles), creating in effect a 33 percent tax bracket during this phase-out period;
- a repeal of the "marriage penalty" deduction;
- expansion of the Dependent Care Tax Credit; and
- retention of most tax preferences given to owner-occupied housing.

For the family, there were both gains and losses. On the positive side, the near doubling of the personal exemption, from $1080 to $2,000, was a significant gain, although the reduction in marginal tax rates (from a top rate of 50 to 28 percent) blunted its effect at the middle income level. Nonetheless, the encouragement to childbearing was real. Whittington, Alms, and Peters predicted in 1987 that this change would result in a direct increase in the U.S. fertility rate of 7.53 births per 1,000 women, aged fifteen to forty-four, by 1990.[43] The real increase turned out to be fairly close to this prediction: 5.5. In addition, indexing the exemption to inflation was a significant achievement, putting a halt to the continued erosion in its value. And elimination of the special deduction for two income couples ended this indirect tax on imputed household income.

On the negative side, though, the Tax Reform Act of 1986, by bringing tax rates down, generally shifted incentives toward the market. One analyst predicted a direct 2.6 percent increase in the labor force participation of wives, due to the tax bill.[44] (The actual increase, by 1990, was even greater: 3.5 percent.) At the same time, the tax benefit for out-of-home childcare, and its indirect tax on the parent-at-home, grew in size and relative importance. The phasing out of the personal exemption at the $71,900 income level abandoned the important principle adopted in 1944 of universality. In practice, this phase-out also became a kind of indirect tax on the children of the relatively well off.

Other negatives could be counted. The significance and probable contemporary negative thrust of housing tax preferences remained unchanged. The so-called "marriage penalty" reappeared in a new form. And an increase in the relative value of the standard deduction for "heads of households" (normally one-parent households) actually enhanced the incentive favoring divorce and an equal division of the children.[45]

In all, the 1986 Act marked the continued erosion of support for families. While fertility was encouraged, marriage faced heightened disincentives, as did the operation of the home economy. More births out of wedlock, more working mothers, and a heightened demand for daycare were the predictable—and actual— results.

In 1991, the bipartisan National Commission on Children, chaired by Senator Jay Rockefeller (D-W.VA), concluded "that further steps are needed to build upon the momentum of pro-family tax reform begun in the late 1980s." Specifically, the Commission recommended the creation of a new, universal $1,000 per child tax credit for all children through age eighteen.[46] Partly in consequence, the summer of 1997 saw Congress give a more open, positive recognition to family claims. Provisions of special relevance to the family in the 1997 tax reform act were:

- The creation of a new Child Tax Credit, worth $400 per child in 1998 and rising to $500 in 1999. Confined to children aged sixteen and under, the credit was phased out for married couples with incomes over $110,000, and for individuals earning above $75,000;
- Educational tax credits to pay for college and university expenses: up to $1,500 for the first two years of college, and up to $2,000 thereafter (with a phase out of the latter provision for married couples earning $80,000 or more, and single taxpayers earning $50,000 or more);
- And an increase in the capital gains tax exclusion to $500,000 (for married couples) on the sale of a principal residence (and $250,000 for singles).

Despite the unfortunate phase out of the Child Tax Credit at higher income levels (writing in the early 1970s, tax theorist Boris Bittker labeled a "vanishing deduction" such as this a "drastic remedy"[47]), this provision was of positive effect, roughly doubling for most families the "tax shelter" impact of each child. The favored treatment given to the capital gains from the sale of a family residence also gave positive encouragement to family capital accumulation. On the other hand, past experience suggested that the new credits for higher education would be of ephemeral utility, quickly absorbed by cost increases at colleges and universities. (And so it happened: college and university costs between 1997 and 2002 rose at four times the rate of general inflation.)

From 1997 to 2000, a Republican-controlled Congress grappled frequently with proposed solutions to the "marriage penalty" created by the abandonment of income splitting in 1969. Several times Congress came close to approving legislation allowing married couples to file their tax returns singly, as if they were unrelated individuals, or jointly—whichever would result in the lower tax burden. This approach would have favored high-income, dual-career families and would have created still stronger incentives for mothers and potential mothers to be in the fulltime labor market. Only last-minute lobbying by The Family Research Council and a few influential individuals stopped this measure from becoming law.[48]

In early 2001, the new George W. Bush administration tried a different approach. Economic advisor Laurence Lindsay shared the view of many pro-business Republicans that the U.S. economy was "running short of willing and able workers." Why? Because high marginal tax rates were "driving skilled married women out of the labor market." When the White House put forward its tax cut recommendations that February, the proposed solution was to go back to the innovation of 1981, and permit the second earner among two-earner married couples to deduct 10 percent of income, up to $30,000. In a narrow sense, this luring of young mothers out-of-the-home would have been good for business. Viewed from the angle of protecting the family economy, though, this approach would have increased the indirect tax on the imputed income of the parent-at-home and pushed more children into daycare.[49]

Fortunately, wiser heads prevailed in Congress. The Economic Growth and Tax Relief Reconciliation Act, signed by President Bush into law in June 2001, embodied a very different remedy to the marriage penalty. The measure doubled the standard deduction for joint filers, relative to singles, and similarly doubled the size of the 15 percent tax bracket for married couples, effective in 2005. Technicalities aside, this was a solid—if sadly deferred—step toward the restoration of income splitting. The marriage penalty within the EITC was also reduced.

More importantly, the same Act raised the value of the Child Tax Credit by 20 percent to $600, effective 2001, with a scheduled increase to $1,000 between 2006 and 2010. Other components with particular effects on families were:

- Immediate rebate checks valued up to $300 for individual filers and $600 for joint filers;
- better treatment for family estates under the federal estate and gift tax system, and its scheduled elimination by 2010;
- gradual reduction of the 28, 31, 36, and 39.6 percent marginal tax brackets to 25, 28, 33, and 35 percent by 2006;
- expansion of the adoption tax credit;
- expansion of the dependent care credit for daycare expenses and creation of a new childcare credit for employers operating daycare centers; and
- increases in allowable contributions to education IRAs, their extension to elementary and secondary education, and a new above-the-line deduction for higher education expenses.

The spring of 2003 saw the increase in the Child Tax Credit to $1,000 made immediate, with rebate checks of $400 per child sent out in the summer. Also speeded up were the cuts in marginal tax brackets.

How, on balance, did traditional families fare? The increase in the value of the child tax credit should be of real benefit to child-rich households. Repairs to existing marriage penalties appeared in ways that should marginally encourage marriage, protect the integrity of the home economy, and slightly benefit the parent-at-home. At the same time, though, reductions in marginal tax rates will favor market labor over home labor, canceling out the earlier effects for upper- and middle-income households. In addition, increases in the tax credits for non-parental daycare continue the federal government's heavy subsidy of institutionalized childcare tied to its absolute refusal to give credit—literally *and* figuratively—to the parents in households who make sacrifices to care for their own small children at home.

Is this a tale, then, of Paradise Gained in 1948, only to be lost two decades later, with haunting echoes into our time?

In part, yes. The tax regime of 1948 was strongly pro-family, the happy combination of real sentiments about the home with the accidents of policymaking. For the first time in one hundred years, America saw three simultaneous social trends: a rise in the marriage rate; a fall in the divorce rate; and a dramatic surge in marital fertility. Favorable public policy played a part in this dramatic turn of events.

And in part, no. The family system of the 1950s, as remarkable as it was, proved unable to sustain itself beyond a single generation. It collapsed in less than a decade, unable to pass its distinctive qualities on to the next generation. Strains in the "breadwinner-homemaker-suburban" model were evident even before negative developments in tax policy could have dramatic impact. Something more than the U.S. Tax Code was incomplete or wrong in this version of Paradise.

That larger story is beyond the scope of this chapter. Suffice it to say that the tests of tax policy relative to the family used in the past—does it favor marriage, discourage divorce, support childrearing, and protect the home—remain valid today, even if the social environment and the policy specifics might differ from those of 1948. The tax reform plan proposed by the Bush administration should be judged against these same principles; so should rival proposals offered by the minority party.

More broadly, the biennial return of policymakers to basic tax reform suggests a deeper problem. Perhaps incremental reform of the income tax will no longer work, the Code too complex, the effects of reform too diffuse. Perhaps more radical policy surgery is needed: a flat tax, for example; or a national consumption tax in place of the federal income tax. If so, the same tests regarding family integrity remain valid, and necessary, to insure that families are served as the fundamental cell of the good society.

Notes

1.   See: Julie A. Nelson, "Tax Reform and Feminist Theory in the United States: Incorporating Human Connection," *Journal of Economic Studies* 18 (No. 5/6, 1991): 19-20; and Anne L. Alstott, "Tax Policy and Feminism: Competing Goals and Institutional Choices," *Columbia Law Review* 96 (Dec. 1996): 2005.
2.   Patricia Cain, "Heterosexual Privilege and the Internal Revenue Code," *University of San Francisco Law Review* 54 (Spring 2000): 465-95.
3.   Laura Ann Mcloskey et al., "A Comparative Study of Battered Women and Their Children in Italy and the United States," *Journal of Family Violence* 17 (2002): 53-74; M. Daly and M. Wilson, "Child Abuse and Other Risks of Not Living with Both Parents," *Ethology and Sociobiology* 6 (1985): 197-209; S.M. Smith, R. Hanson, and S. Noble, "Social Aspects of the Battered Baby Syndrome," in *Child Abuse: Commission and Omission*, eds. J. V. Cook and P. T. Bowles (Toronto: Butterworths, 1980): 205-225.
4.   S. Stack, "The Effect of Domestic/Religious Individualism on Suicide, 1954-1978," *Journal of Marriage and Family* 45 (May 1985): 431-447; G.F.G. Moens et al., "Epidemiological Aspects of Suicide Among the Young in Selected European Countries," *Journal of Epidemiology and Community Health* 42 (1988): 279-285; and S. Stack, "The Effects of Suicide in Denmark, 1961-1980," *The Sociological Quarterly* 31 (1990): 361-368.

5.   "The NHSDA Report: Beliefs Among Youth About Risks from Illicit Drug Use," Office of Applied Studies, Substance Abuse and Mental Health Services Administration [SAMHSA], U.S. Department of Health and Human Services, July 13, 2001, www.samhsa.gov/oas/beliefs.cfmj; I. Chein, D. C. Gerard, R. S. Lee, and E. Rosenfeld, *The Road to H: Narcotics, Delinquency and Social Policy* (New York: Basic Books, 1964); D. B. Kandel, "Drug and Drinking Behavior Among Youth," *Annual Review of Sociology* 6 (1980): 235-285; and J. S. Brook, M. Whiteman, and A. S. Gordon, "Stages of Drug Use in Adolescence: Personality, Peer, and Family Correlates," *Developmental Psychology* 19 (1983): 269-288.

6.   Mark I. Singer and Daniel J. Flannery, "The Relationship Between Children's Threats of Violence and Violent Behaviors," *Archives of Pediatric and Adolescent Medicine* 154 (2000): 785-90; Byron R. Johnson et al., "Does Adolescent Religious Commitment Matter? A Reexamination of the Effects of Religiosity on Delinquency," *Journal of Research in Crime and Delinquency* 38 (2001): 22-40; M. A. Pirog-Good, "Teenage Paternity, Child Support, and Crime," *Social Science Quarterly* 69 (1988): 527-547; J. Figueira-McDonough, "Residence, Dropping Out, and Delinquency Rates," *Deviant Behavior* 14 (1993): 109-132; R. A. Knight and R. A. Prentby, "The Developmental Antecedents and Adult Adaptations of Rapist Subtypes," *Criminal Justice and Behavior* 14 (1987): 403-426; P. Marquis, "Family Disfunction as a Risk Factor in the Development of Antisocial Behavior," *Psychological Reports* 71 (1992): 468-470; and A. J. Beck and S. A. Kline, "Survey of Youth in Custody, 1987," *U.S. Department of Justice, Bureau of Justice Statistics, Special Report* (Washington, DC: U.S. Department of Justice, 1988).

7.   Ronald C. Kessler, Guilherme Borges, and Ellen E. Walters, "Prevalence of Risk Factors for Lifetime Suicide Attempts in the National Comorbidity Survey," *Archives of General Psychiatry* 56 (1999): 617-26; P. M. Prior and B. C. Hayes, "Marital Status and Bed Occupancy in Health and Social Care Facilities in the United Kingdom," *Public Health* 115 (2001): 401-06; Peggy McDonough, Vivienne Walters, and Lisa Strohschein, "Chronic Stress and the Social Patterning of Women's Health in Canada," *Social Science and Medicine* 54 (2002): 767-82; H. Yu and N. Goldman, "Mortality Differentials by Marital Status: An International Comparison," *Demography* 27 (1990): 233-250; E. S. Kisker and N. Goldman, "Perils of Single Life and Benefits of Marriage," *Social Biology* 34 (1990): 135-152; O. Anson, "Living Arrangements and Women's Health," *Social Science and Medicine* 26 (1988): 201-208; and A. Rosengren, H. Wedal, and L. Wilhelmsen, "Marital Status and Mortality in Middle-aged Swedish Men," *American Journal of Epidemiology* 129 (1989): 54-63.

8.   Frans van Poppel, "Children in One-Parent Families: Survival as an Indicator of the Role of Parents," *Journal of Family History* 25 (July 2000): 269-90; Jeffrey T. Cookston, "Parental Supervision and Family Structure: Effects on Adolescent Problem Behaviors," *Journal of Divorce & Remarriage* 31 (1999): 107-27; J. C. Kleinman and S. S. Kessel, "Racial Differences in Low Birth Weight," *New England Journal of Medicine* 317 (1987): 749-753; P. A. Davison, "Family Structure and Children's Health and Well-being: Data from the 1988 National Health Interview Survey on Child Health," Paper presented at the Annual Meeting of the Population Association of America, Toronto, 1990; F. Saucier and A. Ambert, "Parental Marital Status and Adolescents' Health-Risk Behavior," *Adolescence* 18 (1983): 403-411; R. B. Zajonc, "Family Configuration and Intelligence," *Science* 192 (1976): 227-236; J. W. Santrock, "Relation of Type and Onset of Father Absence to Cognitive Development," *Child Development* 43 (1972): 457-469; H. B. Biller, *Paternal Deprivation: Family, School, Sexuality and Society* (Lexington, MA: Lexington Books, 1974); and V.

Marjoribanks, "Environment, Social Class, and Mental Abilities," *Journal of Educational Psychology* 63 (1972): 103-109.

9.   See: Paul R. Amato and Danelle D. DeBaer, "The Transmission of Marital Instability Across Generations: Relationship Skills or Commitment to Marriage?" *Journal of Marriage and Family* 63 (2001): 1038-51; Jane Mauldon, "The Effect of Marital Disruption on Children's Health," *Demography* 27 (Aug. 1990): 431-46; and Ronald L. Simons et al., "Explaining the Higher Incidence of Adjustment Problems Among Children of Divorce Compared with Those in Two-Parent Families," *Journal of Marriage and the Family* 61 (Nov. 1999): 1020-33.

10.   Karen A. Matthews and Brooks B. Gump, "Chronic Work Stress and Marital Dissolution Increase Risk of Post-trial Mortality in Men from the Multiple Risk Factor Intervention Trial," *Archives of Internal Medicine* 162 (2002): 309-15; Patricia A. McManus and Thomas A. DiPrete, "Losers and Winners: The Financial Consequences of Separation and Divorce for Men," *American Sociological Review* 66 (2001): 246-68; and Jack C. Smith, James A. Mercy, and Judith M. Conn, "Marital Status and the Risk of Suicide," *American Journal of Public Health* 78 (1988): 78-80.

11.   A. Sauvy, *General Theory of Population* (New York: Basic Books, 1969); and Julian Simon, *The Economics of Population Growth* (Princeton, NJ: Princeton University Press, 1979).

12.   Siv Gustafsson, "Separate Taxation and Married Women's Labor Supply: A Comparison of West Germany and Sweden," *Journal of Population Economics* 5 (1992): 63-64.

13.   J. G. Hunt and L. Hunt, "The Dualities of Career and Families: New Integrations or New Polarizations?" *Social Problems* 29 (June 1982): 499-510; and H. Rosen, "Tax Illusion and the Labor Supply of Married Women," *The Review of Economics and Statistics* 58 (1976): 170.

14.   Theodore Roosevelt, *Foes of Our Own Household* (New York: George H. Doran Co., 1917): 265-66.

15.   See: Boris Bittker, "Federal Income Taxation and the Family," *Stanford Law Review* 27 (July 1975): 1399-1404.

16.   From: Ernest R. Groves and William Ogburn, *American Marriage and Family Relationships* (New York: Henry Holt, 1928): 106, 121.

17.   See: Leslie Whittington, "Taxes and the Family: The Impact of the Tax Exemption for Dependents on Marital Fertility," *Demography* 29 (May 1992): 220-21.

18.   Bittker, "Federal Taxation and the Family," pp. 1408-11.

19.   Quoted in: Alice Kessler-Harris, "Designing Women and Old Fools: The Construction of the Social Security Amendments of 1939," in Linda Kerber, Alice Kessler-Harris, and Kathryn Kish Sklar, eds., *U.S. History as Women's History* (Chapel Hill: University of North Carolina Press, 1995): 87; more broadly, see: Allan Carlson, "'Sanctif[ying] the Traditional Family': The New Deal and National Solidarity," *The Family in America* 16 (May 2002): 1-12.

20.   *House Ways and Means Committee Report No. 1365*, 78th Congress, 2nd Session, p. 5; quoted in Lawrence H. Seltzer, *The Personal Exemption in the Income Tax* (New York: National Bureau of Economic Research, 1968): 42.

21.   For a detailed treatment of this concept, see: Harold M. Groves, *Federal Tax Treatment of the Family* (Washington, DC: The Brookings Institution, 1963): 56-83.

22.   Gertrude S. Fish, ed., *The Story of Housing* (New York: Macmillan, 1979): 472-475; and D. Laidler, "Income Tax Incentives for Owner-Occupied Housing," in A. C. Harberger and M. J. Bailey, eds., *The Taxation of Income from Capital* (Washington, DC: The Brookings Institution, 1969): 50-64.

23. H. S. Rosen and K. T. Rosen, "Federal Taxes and Home Ownership: Evidence from Time Series," *Journal of Political Economy* 88 (1980): 59-75.

24. Whittington, "Taxes and the Family"; and L. A. Whittington, J. Alan, and H. E. Peters, "Fertility and the Personal Exemption: Implicit Pronatalist Policy in the United States," *The American Economic Review* 80 (June 1990): 545-556.

25. Groves, *Federal Tax Treatments of the Family*, pp. 68-69.

26. David Hartman, "Punishing Families for Wedlock and Children," *The Family in America* 14 (Sept. 2000): 1-8.

27. Groves, *Federal Tax Treatment of the Family*, p. 59.

28. Joseph A. Pechman, *Federal Tax Policy* (Washington, DC: The Brookings Institution, 1966): 83.

29. M. J. Boskin and E. Sheshinski, "Optimal Tax Treatment of the Family: Married Couples," *Journal of Public Economics* 20 (1983): 284.

30. See: Richard L. Meier, "Concerning Equilibrium in Human Population," *Social Problems* 6 (Fall 1958): 163-75.

31. Paul Ehrlich, *The Population Bomb* (New York: Ballantine, 1968): 135-51, 180-81.

32. *Population and the American Future: The Report of the Commission on Population Growth and the American Future* (New York: New American Library, 1972): 122.

33. Eugene Steuerle, "The Tax Treatment of Households of Different Size," in Rudolf G. Penner, ed., *Taxing the Family* (Washington, DC: American Enterprise Institute, 1983): 74.

34. *Report of the Committee on Ways and Means to Accompany H.R. 8363* (Washington, DC: U.S. Government Printing Office, 1963): 24.

35. Bittker, "Federal Income Taxation and the Family," p. 1428.

36. June O'Neill, "Family Issues in Taxation," in Penner, *Taxing the Family*, p. 13.

37. Bittker, "Federal Income Taxation and the Family," pp. 1431-42.

38. On this point, see: A. Blomquist and M. McKee, "Eliminating the 'Marriage Exemption' in the Canadian Income Tax: The Erola Proposal," *Canadian Journal of Economics* 19 (May 1986): 309-317.

39. See: Allan Carlson, *From Cottage to Work Station: The Family's Search for Social Harmony in the Industrial Age* (San Francisco: Ignatius, 1993): 78-84.

40. George Sternlieb and J. W. Hughes, *America's Housing: Prospects and Problems* (New Brunswick, NJ: Center for Urban Policy Research, Rutgers University, 1980): 58-66.

41. Steuerle, "The Tax Treatment of Households of Different Size," p. 75.

42. *The Family: Preserving America's Future. A Report to the President from the White House Working Group on the Family* (Washington, DC: U.S. Department of Education, 1986): 45.

43. Whittington, Alms, and Peters, "Fertility and the Personal Exemption," p. 553.

44. J. A. Hausman and J. M. Poterba, "Household Behavior and the Tax Reform Act of 1986," *Economic Perspectives* 1 (Summer 1987): 108.

45. Noted in Thomas J. Espenshade and J. J. Minarik, "Demographic Implications of the 1986 U.S. Tax Reform," *Population and Development Review* 13 (March 1987): 119.

46. *Beyond Rhetoric: A New American Agenda for Children and Families. Final Report of The National Commission on Children* (Washington, DC: U.S. Government Printing Office, 1991): 94.

47. Bittker, "Federal Income Taxation and the Family," p. 1452.

48. See: Allan Carlson and David Blankenhorn, "Marriage and Taxes," *The Weekly Standard* (Feb. 9, 1998).

49. David Blankenhorn and Allan Carlson, "Marriage Penalties," *The Weekly Standard* (Feb. 26, 2001).

7

Love is Not Enough: Toward the Recovery of a Family Economics

A temptation in our time—perhaps in every time—is the suppression of uncomfortable truths in favor of unthreatening myths and pseudo-solutions. We can see this process of distortion in contemporary talk about the relationship of the family to economic life.

On the political left, the dominant conversation on these matters today concerns so-called "work-family conflicts." Authors such as Jody Heymann[1] and Theda Skocpol[2] argue that with most able bodied adults now at work, a serious "care giving deficit has emerged," with both children and the elderly abandoned to inadequate institutional care. Largely ignoring the home, the government-centered solutions offered by these authors include more federal subsidies for infant and toddler daycare, longer school days and years, mandatory paid parental insurance, and greater funding for elder care centers. Management professors Stewart Friedman and Jeffrey Greenhaus,[3] for their part, call for a different kind of revolution, emphasizing that "To create options that help make allies of work and family...we need to change the traditional gender roles." Women, they say, must be drawn more completely into "the *brave new world* of twenty-first century careers"; men must be retrained to perform more child- and elder care; and children should be placed in "innovative summer camps" designed to create a new family order.

Among contemporary conservatives, meanwhile, there is authentic attachment to "the traditional family." All the same, conservative efforts at welfare reform still aim primarily at putting welfare mothers to work and their children in state subsidized daycare—peculiar ways to save already damaged families, I sometimes think. And the 2000 Republican Party platform proudly embraced the once-radical feminist goal of full, government-enforced gender equality in jobs, promotions, and contracts—a process that in practice, as I will explain, has and will discourage marriage and reward divorce.

What is the truth about the relation of the family to the economy? Any answer must start by underscoring the vast consequences for the family brought on by that event we call the Industrial Revolution.

Before the rise of modern industry, let us remember, virtually the whole of humankind lived in family-centered economies. The *family* was the locus of most productive activity, whether on largely self-sufficient family farms or in small family shops. In the United States of America, circa 1800, about 90 percent of the free population were farmers; most of the remaining ten percent were artisans or shopkeepers. Even these town dwellers normally kept a kitchen garden, chickens, and a cow. Husbands and wives *relied on* each other, *needed* each other, *shared* with each other, so that their small family enterprises might succeed. They specialized in their daily tasks, according to their respective skills. Marriage was still true here to its historic definition: a *union* of the sexual *and* the economic. Life for these Americans was little different from that of the hundreds of generations that had gone before. In a recent essay, anthropologist Hugh Brody ably captures the tone of this family-centric order:

> A family is busy in the countryside. Mother is making bread, churning butter, attending to hens and ducks…preparing food for everyone. Father is in the fields, ploughing the soil, cutting wood, fixing walls, providing sustenance. Children explore and play and help and sit at the family table. Grandma or grandpa sit in a chair by the fire. Every day is long and filled with the activities of this family…. *The family in its farm is the family where it belongs*. A place of integration where work, play, childhood and age all share a safe and secure space.[4]

The industrial revolution of the nineteenth century tore through this settled way of life.[5] There were large material gains, to be sure. Industrial production, using an exaggerated division of labor, produced standardized goods at a cheaper price. Inherited ways and community restraints that had limited options retreated before new understandings of freedom.

Relative to the *family as an institution*, though, the story was radically different. Most dramatically, the family household was dethroned as the center of productive activity. The process usually began with the making of cloth, as the home spinning wheel and loom gave way to water or steam powered machines in the factory. But quickly, virtually everything once homemade followed: from shoes and furniture to vegetables, bread, and meat. Cash exchanges displaced the altruistic exchanges of the family. Meanwhile, education moved from home control to regimentation by the state in schools organized on an industrial model. "Child protection," another family function, passed to government as well.

The formula was simple and precise: as the industrial sector grew, the family weakened. By the end of the nineteenth century, the function-rich family had become nearly *function-less*. The feminist author Charlotte Perkins Gilman, in her 1899 book *Women and Economics*, saw the tasks of the once productive family reduced even by then to only three: cooking; cleaning; and early childcare. She saw no reason why these three functions could not be industrialized as well, and she proceeded—again, back in 1899—to lay out visions for a *fast-food industry* where people would pick up their pre-cooked meals in bags at a window; for *Kindercare* at commercial daycare centers; and for commercial cleaning services, a.k.a. The Merry Maids.[6]

The new industrial order also divided families into their component parts. Mothers, fathers, and children were each pulled into the ranks of wage laborer, according to their different aptitudes. Family bonds became an obstruction to this efficient allocation of labor. The individual, standing alone, became the ideal worker. In consequence, men and women, parents and children needed each other much less than before. In the words of the English essayist, G. K. Chesterton: "[The family] is literally being torn in pieces, in that the husband may go to one factory, the wife to another, and the child to a third. Each will become the servant of a separate financial group, which is more and more gaining the political power of a feudal group. But whereas feudalism received the loyalty of families, the lords of the new servile state will receive only the loyalty of individuals: that is, of lonely men and even of lost children."[7]

Advertising became another vehicle for deconstructing the family economy. It worked to whet appetites for more industrially produced goods, to imply that remaining forms of family production were inadequate, and to draw family members still further into the emerging world of consumerism. Indeed, the measures of economic growth came to rest to a considerable degree on the steady transfer of ever more tasks from the uncounted household economy to the fully accounted industrial orbit.

Still, religious leaders, reformers, labor leaders, and working families themselves mounted a last great counterattack. They sought to put barriers around the home, to limit the spread of the industrial principle, to preserve some domain of family autonomy in the new economic order. This is how we should understand, I think, the old regime of the "family wage." Under its sway, the industrial sector would be allowed to claim only one family member per household— normally the father, who would receive a family-sustaining wage in return. Children would leave the factories, and so would their mothers, to return to their homes and salvage some aspects of family living: reproduction; childcare; and shared consumption. Under this regime, single women would obviously claim a smaller wage, suitable to one person. Widows and orphans would be entitled to a public pension. As the labor chieftain John L. Lewis explained the principle: "Normally, a husband and father should be able to earn enough to support his family…. I am *violently opposed* to a system which, by degrading the earnings of adult males, makes it economically necessary for wives and children to become supplementary wage earners."[8]

This "family wage" system, I need underscore, was also popular. A 1936 Gallup Poll asked if wives should work if their husbands had jobs. *Eighty-two* percent said "No," leading George Gallup to observe that he had finally "discovered an issue on which voters are about as solidly united as on any subject imaginable—including sin and hay fever."[9]

At a loftier level, family sociologists called this new system a "companionship family." As industrially organized entities—corporate, governmental, and even charitable—completed their absorption of the old family functions of production, education, recreation, and child protection, the "companionship family" would refocus on psychological intimacy, democracy, and *love*, or—in the words from 1945 of sociologists Ernest Burgess and Henry J. Locke—on "the mutual affection, the sympathetic understanding, and the comradeship of its members."[10]

Did this model succeed? For a time, roughly from 1935 to 1965, the answer could be *yes*. The "companionship family," built on "the working father/homemaking mother" model, recovered a kind of *division-of-labor*. Men would focus on wage-earning work outside the home. Women would specialize in the "homemaking" tasks of childcare, cooking, cleaning, and informed consumption. As Nobel laureate Gary Becker has shown in his now classic work, *A Treatise on the Family*, a marriage represents real economic gain only when husband and wife specialize. In pre-industrial, agrarian times, this specialization would normally follow that described earlier by Hugh Brody: the husband in the field; the wife in the kitchen, garden, and chicken house. Under the "companionship model," a new balance was struck, one where the *marriage* would again create an economic partnership greater than the sum of its parts.[11]

This model took firmest root in the United States, encouraged in part by new governmental actions: tax measures such as "income splitting" for married couples that favored homemakers; housing policies that encouraged young couples to purchase suburban homes; and social welfare policies crafted during the New Deal that favored the "family wage for fathers/homemaking for mothers" model.[12] The "family wage" paid to fathers actually *expanded*, evidenced in a widening average differential between men's pay and women's pay. Driving this was a growing and largely voluntary job segregation by gender, where custom reserved the higher paid jobs for men with wives and children at home.[13]

And there were measurable results: where U.S. marriage and fertility rates had fallen sharply between 1900 and 1934, they began climbing again in 1935 and soared upward ten years later. A marriage boom occurred, followed by the more famous "Baby Boom." College-educated women, a hefty number with degrees in the popular field of "home economics," were in the vanguard of this family renewal, with their fertility more than doubling. The creation of new family households occurred at a record pace, and the proportion of Americans living in married-couple households reached an historical high. Between 1947 and 1960, the divorce rate reversed a hundred-year trend and steadily declined. The average age of first marriage fell *below* twenty-one for women, another unprecedented figure, and these same women embraced domesticity and homemaking with purposeful commitment. The schools overflowed with children, and America seemed once again to be a youthful, child-centered, family-oriented land.

But love was not enough to hold this restored family-centered world together. Challenges grew evident in the mid-1960s; ten years later, the American family system was in full-blown crisis. The birth rate tumbled sharply, to but half its former level. By 1976, U.S. fertility was 15 percent below the zero growth level. The divorce rate climbed 150 percent in the same period, while the proportion of births outside of wedlock soared. The marriage rate also began a steady retreat, particularly among men and women under the age of thirty.

What caused this return *with a vengeance* to the family disorders of the early decades of the twentieth century? Part of the answer lies in the continued desire by the industrial sector for women's work, as a way to expand the labor pool and hold wages down. In 1955, for example, at the very height of the Baby Boom and the restored domesticity centered on the suburbs, Columbia University and the Dwight Eisenhower administration convened a Conference on the Effective Use of Womanpower. Speakers at this meeting called for a new agenda for women's work, including increased formal education and training, the discouragement of early marriage, and the movement of women into scientific and technical jobs. According to the feminist historian Alice Kessler-Harris, this meeting "reflected a major turnabout in official thinking.... [S]lowly a new mentality was dawning."[14]

At the same time, neo-Malthusians who looked with horror at the baby-booming suburbs plotted "large-scale attempts to manipulate family size desires, even rather stealthily."[15] The most effective way to increase the number of sterile adults, according to one Malthusian planner, was to move women into jobs that required geographic mobility and so made a stable home and community life impossible: jobs such as airline piloting, engineering, sales, and fire fighting. Easy divorce would also create more sterile marriages, he reasoned.[16]

In addition, U.S. federal policy shifted strongly against the child-rich, married-couple family. The Kennedy tax cut of 1962 violated the principle behind "income splitting" and created the first of many "marriage penalties" in the tax code. By the late 1960s, the federal income tax burden was rapidly shifting *away* from corporations, unmarried individuals, and the childless *onto* the backs of married couples with children. Indeed, the larger the family, the greater the growing tax burden.[17]

Meanwhile, a curious development occurred during passage of The Civil Rights Act of 1964. As originally crafted by The Lyndon Johnson White House, Title VII of the Bill prohibited job discrimination only in the areas of "race, color, religion, or national origin." Everyone knew that its overriding—if indirect—purpose was to help African American men gain better jobs, so they might become more stable husbands, fathers, and breadwinners, and so reverse the rising tide of broken homes and illegitimacy in black neighborhoods. Yet during the heat of debate, southern segregationists—the so-called "Dixiecrats"—offered an amendment to add the word "sex" to Title VII. They hoped, it appears, to scuttle the civil rights bill through this measure; or, failing that, to redirect its focus from African American men to white women. Enough equity feminists were on the House floor that day to join with the Dixiecrats to pass the amendment. While hearings were never held on the purpose or meaning of this change, the "sex" amendment survived a conference with the Senate and became law.[18]

For a few years, the import of the "sex" amendment to Title VII was unclear. But in 1967, President Johnson issued an executive order that prohibited all forms of sex discrimination in hiring and promotion among federal contractors and mandated "affirmative," "result oriented" efforts.[19] The most important effect was to make "job segregation by gender"—the foundation of America's informal family wage regime—illegal. Characterizations such as "men's jobs" and "women's jobs" were quickly suppressed, and the consequences soon grew apparent. The real wages of men declined by 30 percent over the next two decades; the real wages of women rose slightly.

Overall, family households now needed two incomes to hold their own, or to show some real gain. And this meant, in turn, that the division of labor between men and women created earlier in the twentieth century began to crumble. As women moved into the paid labor force on terms equal to those of men, they became more *like men* in function. In consequence, the economic logic of marriage blurred. There would be little gain from a union of equals. While "specialization" continued its forced march through the industrial sector, it withered within the home. A falling marriage rate, rising divorce, tumbling marital fertility, and widespread cohabitation were the predictable results.

At a still deeper level, I would also underscore that the restored family economy of the celebrated 1950s, the family of the suburban boom, was actually fragile. With rare exceptions, few family functions lost to the industrial order during the prior hundred years were brought home. Charlotte Perkins Gilman's list of remaining family functions from 1899—cooking, cleaning, and early childcare—still held for the most part in 1957. Nothing had been added. While erosion of the family's economic base had been slowed, for a time, it had not been reversed, and the suburban model of the 1950s was ill equipped to withstand the ideological challenges it faced a decade later. As the Kentucky poet and essayist Wendell Berry has put it in his book *What Are People For?*:

> [W]e must be careful to see that the old cultural centers of home and community were made vulnerable to this [industrial] invasion by their failure as economies. If there is no household or community economy, then family members and neighbors are no longer useful to one another. When people are no longer useful to one another, then the centripetal force of family and community fails, and people fall into dependence on exterior economies and organizations.

Turning specifically to education, Berry continued: "The local schools no longer serve the local community; they serve the government's economy and the economy's government."[20]

In short, the troubling and difficult message is: marriages will *not* be strengthened on a society wide basis, nor will families, unless the *economic logic* for entering a marriage and rearing children increases. This might be called an economic "fact of life" that no amount of wishful thinking, self-deception, or mass-deception can overcome.

Moreover, it is highly unlikely that something approximating the family order of the 1935-65 era could be reconstructed. To phrase it mildly, there is no popular consensus today in favor of a "family wage" regime resting on job segregation by gender, which served as the economic foundation for that social order. Just as important, the family system of those "Happy Days" was—despite some signs of strength—vulnerable, something of a one-generation wonder. We need to do better.

Toward that end, I want to suggest three alternate strategies for renewing the family economy in the early twenty-first century.

The first strategy is the creative use of tax policy. "Income splitting" for married couples should be restored as the law of the land; measures adopted in 2001 to tackle the "marriage penalty" were but tentative first steps here. The relatively new child tax credit, recently increased to $1,000, should be increased again to at least $2,500 per child and indexed to inflation. Currently phased out as children reach age sixteen, it should be continued through age eighteen. The existing income limit for eligibility should be scrapped as well. Meanwhile, the Dependent Care Tax Credit—now available only to working parents who place their children in substitute commercial care—should be transformed into a universal "preschool" credit fixed at an extra $2500, and available to *all* parents with children under age five, most especially including parents caring fulltime for their small children at home. If these tax cuts required offsetting "revenue en-hancements," somewhat greater progressivity gained through extra tax brackets would be an acceptable "pro-family" strategy; under "income splitting," it turns out, progressivity actually favors the married couple household.[21] Taken together, these changes would encourage marriage, *specialization within households*, and the birth of children without violating the contemporary legal imperative of gender equality.

The second strategy for renewing the home economy is to bring important family functions, lost in the past to outside agency, back within the family circle. The model for doing this is home school-ing. This revolution in education began for varied reasons: some parents were disturbed by the regimentation of conventional school-ing, based as it was on an industrial model; others by the moral vacuum growing within the public schools. Viewed historically, though, home schooling represents the return of a vital family func-tion to its natural sphere. While the educational results for children can be impressive, the effects on the family as an institution are more important. Once begun, home schooling inspires a complete reordering of family relationships. Priorities change in profound ways. Relative to the economic issues I have described, home schooling encourages and rewards specialization by husband and wife, which strengthens the marriages involved. These "refunctionalized" fami-lies do, indeed, grow stronger as a result,[22] and they commonly look for other functions to bring home, such as vegetable gardening or a small family business.

The third strategy for renewing the home economy is the building of *intentional communities*. To convey my meaning here, I want briefly to tell you the story of one such community. In 1973, a pair of young Southern Baptist pastors from Texas went to New York City and started a storefront church in "Hell's Kitchen," one of Manhattan's seedier neighborhoods, characterized by prostitution, drugs, and crime. Over the next ten years, these pastors pulled to-gether a diverse congregation: white, black, Latino; lapsed Catho-lics and Protestants; the never-churched; and converted Jews. They taught the virtues of self-reliance, and the members of their congre-gation turned, in succession, to *home births*, *breastfeeding*, *home schooling*, *home churches*, and *urban gardens*. In the early 1980s they resolved on the need for more space. About 150 moved to a beautiful Colorado valley. Reaching into their Anabaptist heritage, they sought lessons from the Amish on how a community might master or control the pressures of industrialization. Husbands and wives specialized in their daily work according to their gifts. Learning to use work horses, they farmed some of their land as a group, not because it made good sense from a strict calculation of efficiency, but because it made them better neighbors. About a dozen years ago, the community moved to central Texas, settling on land along The Brazo de Dios, or "Arms of God," River. Taking the name Heritage Homesteads, this religious community now numbers about 700 on this land, with thousands of associates in the Austin area and Monterrey, Mexico.[23] While the details will necessarily vary, this is a model of economic cooperation that can be, and is being, replicated in other places throughout our land. There is one qualification, though: the American experience strongly suggests that *only* those communities resting on a vital religious faith have a real chance of success.

Creative tax policy; bringing vital tasks or functions home; creating intentional communities: it is in these ways that we might, in our time, succeed in taming the industrial impulse so that it becomes the *servant*, not the master, of families.

Notes

1.   See: Jody Heymann, *The Widening Gap: Why America's Working Families Are in Jeopardy and What Can Be Done About It* (New York: Basic Books, 2000).

2.   Theda Skocpol, *The Missing Middle: Working Families and the Future of American Social Policy* (New York: W.W. Norton, 2000).

3.   Stewart Friedman and Jeffrey Greenhaus, *Work and Family: Allies or Enemies?* (New York: Oxford University Press, 2000).

4.   Hugh Brody, "Nomads and Settlers," in Anthony Barnett and Roger Scruton, eds., *Town and Country* (London: Vintage, 1999): 3-4. Emphasis added.

5.   One classic interpretation of this change is: Karl Polanyi, *The Great Transformation* (Boston: Beacon Press, 1944).

6.   Charlotte Perkins Gilman, *Women and Economics: A Study of the Economic Relation Between Men and Women as a Factor in Social Evolution*, ed., Carl N. Degler (New York: Harper & Row, 1966 [1899]).

7.   G. K. Chesterton, *The Superstition of Divorce*, in *Collected Works* Vol. IV, *Family, Society, Politics* (San Francisco: Ignatius Press, 1987): 259-60.

8.   Quoted in Suzanne Mettler, *Dividing Citizens: Gender and Federalism in New Deal Public Policy* (Ithaca: Cornell University Press, 1998): 189.

9.   Susan Ware, *Holding Their Own: American Women in the 1930s* (Boston: Twayne Publishers, 1982): 27.

10.   E. W. Burgess and H. J. Locke, *The Family* (New York: American Book Company, 1945): 651.

11.   See: Gary S. Becker, *A Treatise on the Family* (Cambridge, MA: Harvard University Press, 1981); and Robert T. Michael and Gary S. Becker, "On the New Theory of Consumer Behavior," *Swedish Journal of Economics* 75 (1973): 379-96.

12.   See, most recently: Allan Carlson, "'Sanctif[ying] the Traditional Family': The New Deal and National Solidarity," *The Family in America* 16 (May 2002): 1-12.

13.   See: A. C. Carlson, "Gender, Children, and Social Labor: Transcending the 'Family Wage' Dilemma," *Journal of Social Issues* 52 (No. 3 1996): 143-48.

14.   Alice Kessler-Harris, *Out to Work: A History of Wage Earning Women in the United States* (New York: Oxford University Press, 1982): 308.

15.   Edward Pohlman, "Mobilizing Social Pressures Toward Small Families," *Eugenics Quarterly* 13 (Spring 1966): 122-26.

16.   Richard L. Meier, "Concerning Equilibrium in Human Population," *Social Problems* 6 (Fall 1958): 163-75.

17.   For more on this, see: Allan Carlson, "Toward a Theory of Family Taxation," in Henry Cavanna, ed., *The New Citizenship of the Family* (Aldershot, England: Ashgate, 2000): 123-24.

18.   Paul Adam Blanchard, "Insert the Word 'Sex': How Segregationists Handed Feminists a 1964 'Civil Rights' Victory Against the Family," *The Family in America* 12 (March 1998): 1-8.

19.   See: Donald Allen Robinson, "Two Movements in Pursuit of Equal Opportunity," *Signs: Journal of Women in Culture and Society* 4 (No. 3, 1979): 427.

20.   Wendell Berry, *What Are People For?* (San Francisco: North Point Press, 1990): 164.

21.   Carlson, "Toward a Theory of Family Taxation," p. 122.

22.   This strength is evidenced through higher fertility and fewer divorces. See: J. Gary Knowles, Maralee Mayberry, and Brian D. Ray, "An Assessment of Home Schools in Nevada, Oregon, Utah, and Washington: Implications for Public Education and a Vehicle for Informed Policy Decisions: Summary Report," U.S. Department of Education Field Initiated Research Project (Grant #R117E90220), submitted to U.S. Department of Education, December 24, 1991.

23.   See: *A Glimpse of Brazos de Dios* (Elm Mott, TX: Heritage Homesteads, n.d.); and Lana Robertson, "Simple Gifts," *Texas Highways* 43 (Nov. 1996): 36-41.

8

A Fresh Vision of the Multigenerational Family

A time bomb lying within the federal budget in the decades ahead is the cost of long-term care (or LTC) for the frail elderly. Greater longevity and the aging of the Baby Boomers are the demographic factors driving this change. The census of 2000 counted 4.3 million Americans aged eighty-five and over. By 2030, that number should grow to 7.7 million. Two decades later, in 2050, it should almost double again to an estimated 14.5 million Americans. The federal government expects the number of nursing home residents, which reached 1.65 million in 1999, to climb to 2.5 million by 2020 and to 4.5 million by 2060. The number of functionally disabled persons aged sixty-five or over living in community-based care should reach *15.2* million in that latter year; again, about three times today's number.[1]

Individual costs should also soar. In recent years, the LTC industry has recorded cost increases averaging between 6 and 8 percent, over three times the overall inflation rate. By the year 2030, the American Council of Life Insurers predicts LTC costs to rise fourfold: *adult daycare*, from $50 per day in 1999 to $220 per day (or $56,100 per year); *home health aide visits*, from $61 per daily visit to $260 per visit (or $68,000 per year); *assisted living facilities*, from $25,000 per year to $109,300; and *nursing homecare*, from an average of $44,000 per year to *$190,000 per year in 2030.*[2]

When these rising human numbers and costs are factored together, the results are numbing. Nursing home costs alone, which totaled $72.8 billion in 1999, would soar to $571.8 billion by 2030: a staggering sevenfold increase. Much of this burden would fall, inevitably, on government Medicaid and Medicare entitlements.

Was this situation inevitable? Even factoring in gains in longevity, the answer is certainly *no*. For the whole of human history, until the middle decades of the twentieth century, the care of the frail elderly came from their family or their neighbors: what social welfare analysts now call "informal care." The common American assumption, inherited from colonial times, reinforced by the Founding era, and continuing through the 1920s, was that each true family represented a continuum, with a past, a present, and a future—a living bond between the generations of a family. Writing fifty-five years ago, the renegade economist Ralph Borsodi ably summarized the *ideal* vision of this vital family and the obligations it conveyed:

> This [family] continuum is a corporate entity; with a corporate name, corporate values, corporate history and traditions, corporate customs and habits, corporate reputation and good will; with a corporate estate, real and personal; composed not only of its present membership, but a membership in the past, and a membership in the future, of which the members in being and in occupation—the living family group—are representatives, entitled to the usufruct [or the use] of the family's corporate heritage, but obligated, as trustees for their posterity, to the conservation of that heritage.[3]

Again, this true family was at least three-generational and assumed care for its frail elderly as a matter of duty and as an expression of its continuity. Indeed, adults in their productive years still understood in some manner the need they had to marry and successfully rear children themselves so as to provide for their own security. The intentionally childless broke the great chain of heritage and also put themselves at risk.

But is not all this part of the myth of the three-generational family? Did not industrialization and urbanization scatter families and end significant family-centered care?

At least from the perspective of 1929, nearly a hundred years into the industrial revolution, the answers were *no*. In all states, law and custom continued to reinforce the obligation of adult children to provide for their elderly parents when the latter could no longer provide for themselves. Simply put, there was no "crisis" in long-term care. It is true that the normally unpleasant "poorhouses" and "poor farms," usually run at the municipal and county levels, found a growing proportion of their residents to be in the "never married" and/or "childless" categories. But few people actually lived in these places: perhaps 50,000 during the 1920s, about .67 of 1 percent of those aged sixty-five and over. This was hardly a social crisis.[4] As historian W. Andrew Achenbaum concludes in his definitive work, *Old Age in the New Land*, absent the Great Depression, the family-centered approach to elder care would probably have continued into the future. The pressure for change was simply not strong enough, circa 1929, to suppress the inherited American values of family integrity and personal responsibility. Achenbaum argues that most workers would have remained in the labor force as long as possible, secured their own retirements through savings and private annuities, and relied on their children, other family members, and their communities for back-up security.[5]

But the Great Depression did come, with record levels of unemployment, widespread bank failures and the loss of savings, the bankruptcy of numerous insurance firms carrying private annuities, and so on. Even so, patterns of elder care remained largely unchanged. As the Committee on Economic Security, charged by President Franklin Roosevelt with crafting a new system, admitted in 1935: "children, friends and relatives have borne and still carry the major costs of supporting the aged."[6] Yet, true to its charge, the Committee went on to recommend the creation of a new system of publicly financed social insurance for old age and disability.

It is important to note that in crafting this new order, the Committee embraced certain assumptions about the American future:

First, the Committee members assumed that the American birthrate would steadily decline. In a widely cited essay, also referenced in the Committee's report, the noted demographer P. K. Whelpton predicted in 1930 that U.S. fertility, which had recently fallen near to the zero growth level, would tumble still further, with "no stopping...place...indicated on the surface." This pointed to a rapid alteration in the age structure of the United States that made imperative an "overhaul" of American social institutions to care for the sharply growing proportion of elderly.[7]

Second, the Committee on Economic Security held that the American family was inevitably weakening. The volume *Recent Social Trends in the United States*, commissioned by President Herbert Hoover, appeared in early 1933. Its impact was large. Behind a scientific veneer, though, lurked a technocratic and socialist ideology. Relative to the family, University of Chicago sociologist William F. Ogburn argued from his "functionalist" angle that American families were in irreversible decay. "Working wives" and the turn to professionals were signs of this change. Already, American homes had shed virtually every function that they had once held. All of social evolution pushed toward "the individualization of the members of the family" and the expansion of "society's" role, meaning government's role. In line with this, Ogburn saw *no future prospects* for significant levels of family care for the elderly.[8] This function, too, must pass to government-paid experts.

Third, the architects of the Social Security system assumed *that economic stagnation would be permanent and the number of future jobs limited.* This made it all the more urgent to create Social Security pensions for the relatively old, in order to lure them into retirement and give their jobs to younger workers.[9]

Tellingly, *none* of these assumptions proved to be true. For example, the very next year—1936—saw the U.S. birthrate start to climb again; by 1947, the Baby Boom was in full swing and would last until 1963. Nor did family care of the elderly disappear. As late as 1982, *78 percent* of functionally impaired elderly persons living in a community relied *exclusively* on the unpaid, informal care of family members, friends, and neighbors.[10] Finally, relative to the number of jobs, there were 135.2 million Americans in the civilian work force in 2000, up *350 percent* since 1935. The real increase in Gross Domestic Product during this time was of a magnitude of 2000 percent.

All the same, the three assumptions I noted—declining fertility, weakening and functionless families, and economic stagnation—worked their way into the very operation of Social Security. Over the decades, they gained a life and influence of their own, and began *producing the very effects* that they had assumed.

To focus on how this happened, I want to turn to an unusual source: Karl Marx. One of the doctrines in Marx's scheme was his belief that the internal contradictions of capitalism would inevitably bring the system down. As he wrote in *Capital*: "Capitalist production begets, with the inexorability of a law of nature, its own negation." As citizens of 2002, we know that Marx made *grave miscalculations* and that it would be the Marxist regimes of the Soviet Union and Eastern Europe that would beat capitalist societies to history's graveyard. Nonetheless, Marx's concept of a system's "internal contradictions" remains a useful intellectual tool. Specifically, I believe it can help us understand the deep flaws to be found in America's policy regarding care for the elderly.

Indeed, I assert that there are *five* "internal contradictions" to elder care in America: (1) the *institutional* contradiction; (2) the *altruism* contradiction; (3) the *family* contradiction; (4) the *demographic* contradiction; and (5) the *efficiency* contradiction. These aspects of the system have not only hurt the very persons who are supposed to be helped; they endanger the good order of society.

First, there is the "institutional" contradiction. The architects of the new Social Security system were firm on one point: there would be no support for aged persons living in the homes, farms, and almshouses run by counties and municipalities. A 1925 Department of Labor report had found that "dilapidation, inadequacy, and even indecency" characterized these institutions, compounded by the "[i]gnorance, unfitness, and complete lack of comprehension" of their managing personnel.[11] Title I of the Social Security Act of 1935 created a federal program of grants-in-aid to the states for old age assistance (or OAA). Designed as a non-contributory, means-tested pension program, OAA would support the impoverished elderly until the new, contributory Social Security system could be fully implemented. Relative to the future, the plan contained one key clause: OAA benefits could *not* be paid to any "inmate of a public institution." The effect of this, *as intended*, was to drive most municipal homes, county farms, and almshouses out of business. But there was *an unintended effect*, as well. Just as the frail elderly without family support were being turned out of the despised public homes, they suddenly had a little OAA cash in their pockets. With few choices as to where to go, they began turning out of necessity to the privately-run "rest homes" and "convalescent homes" that existed on the margins of the health care world in the 1930s. Most of these were also poorly staffed, dilapidated, and unsafe. The exploitation and abuse of residents in them was common. Nonetheless, since they were clearly not "public institutions," these proprietary homes found a new federally inspired revenue stream, and new life.

In short, the "nursing home industry" was born as "an inadvertent,"[12] unanticipated byproduct of poorly thought-out public policy. Over time, the OAA grants were replaced by other federal programs, eventually Medicaid and Medicare. The industry grew in size and political clout. A 1954 amendment to the Hill-Barton Act did try to "medicalize" the nursing home business, providing federal grants to public and non-profit entities to construct nursing homes. All the same, proprietary homes run for profit remained dominant in the field. In 1999, they still numbered 12,000, or two-thirds of all nursing homes. Although ownership was private, *three-quarters* of nursing home revenue still came from federal and state sources, making the nursing home business as much a "government industry" as, say, Lockheed or Grumman Aircraft.[13] In short, the Social Security Act of 1935 aimed at freeing the frail elderly from institutionalization in locally-run homes and farms, but ended up reinstitutionalizing them in a vastly larger and more politically potent industry, one that proved to be beyond the scope of effective local regulation.[14]

The second innate problem found in old age care in America is the "altruism contradiction." Advocates for the modern welfare state argue that their system rests on the principles of altruism and reason. Unlike informal care, they say, the state alternative is fair, compassionate, and rational.

In practice, though, the welfare system ends up tangled in a web of stupidity and irrationality. Long-term care, for example, is available under Medicare for only limited reasons and for a limited number of days. Medicaid provides most government-paid LTC, but only if the recipient is first impoverished. The actual results range from the destruction of small- to middle-sized family patrimonies—a government-inspired end of "the family's corporate heritage" described by Borsodi—to "planned impoverishment," where wealthier persons with good lawyers formally divest themselves of assets in order to stand "impoverished" at the Medicaid door.

More broadly, the "rational" welfare state succeeds only as its citizens behave in irrational fashion. While making limitless promises, called entitlements, the system can succeed only as citizens restrain their claims and continue to behave as though the public programs did not exist: for example, with most of the frail elderly still drawing their care from informal, unpaid sources. However, the system itself penalizes these very persons—givers and receivers alike—for their altruistic behavior. In effect, public authorities reward families who turn their elderly members over to public care and penalize, through taxation, those families providing informal care. As the Danish analyst Bent Andersen has explained:

> The rationally founded welfare state has a built-in contradiction: if it is to fulfill its intended function, its citizens must refrain from exploiting to the fullest its services and provisions—that is, they must behave irrationally, motivated by informal social controls, which, however, tend to disappear as the welfare system grows.[15]

And so, a system crafted in the name of reason and altruism ends up penalizing altruism and relying on irrationality to survive.

My third, and related, indictment can be called the "family contradiction." The public long-term care system assumes weakened, scattered, and unwilling families and offers its compassionate arms as a substitute. In fact, as already noted, two-thirds of disabled elderly persons living in community currently receive *all* of their assistance from informal sources, *primarily* family members.[16] Even among persons who enter a nursing home, the existence of a daughter triples the possibility of a "live exit," revealing nursing-home jargon for a return home by the patient; the existence of a living spouse raises the possibility of "live exit" an extraordinary 26 times.[17] This informal care, according to independent analysts, is "more flexible, usually more caring, and more reciprocal."[18] Moreover, arguments that broad social changes such as the entry of women into the labor market doom informal care keep running into very different realities. According to one careful recent report:

> Many women work and provide informal care at the same time. In addition, it is often overlooked that about one third of all informal caregivers are themselves elderly, and often retired. Finally, mortality trends suggest that more elderly women in the future will have their husbands with them longer.... [M]ale spouses have been shown to be as equally committed to caring for their wives as female spouses are committed to their husbands.[19]

In short, the much-advertised "dwindling supply" of future informal family caregivers need not occur.

However, in a perverse way, this "dwindling supply" is created by government policy itself. In a careful study of Medicaid homecare benefits, for example, Susan Ettner of Harvard Medical School found new government aid *driving out* informal family care. Specifically: "...the Medicaid subsidies induced a substantial replacement of voluntary care by family and friends *by formal paid care* for services that are non-medical in nature."[20] With burning clarity, we see here how a Medicaid project justified by inaccurate assumptions actually creates the problem it claims to solve: diminished family-centered care. The net result is less loving and less personal care for the frail elderly; the deterioration of local community; and higher public expenditures.

The fourth internal problem can be called "the demographic contradiction" of social insurance. Simply put, publicly provided old age, health, and LTC social insurance *rewards* the childless and *penalizes* those who raise children. And since "pay-as-you-go" social insurance is, in essence, a pyramid scheme, requiring new babies who will grow up to be new workers who can be taxed to pay for the system in the future, we can also see how social insurance tends to undermine its own foundations.

Consider the situation of rational, income-maximizing twenty-two-year-olds in the year 2002. As they look to the future, they see their foolish older siblings and acquaintances who married and produced children. These irrational people are now investing most of their income in their children, driving old minivans, living in heavily mortgaged homes, eating tuna casserole, and calling a day-at-the-beach "our vacation." They also can see that if they remain childless, they will have substantial amounts of extra future income that can be spent on fine automobiles, elegant apartments, gourmet meals, and lavish vacations in Greece, Cancun, and Tahiti. And when old age comes, the social insurance system *treats both choices exactly the same*: the frivolous childless and the responsible childrich receive the same pension, and the same access to long-term care under Medicare and Medicaid rules. The system conveys a message: "Children are expensive, time-consuming, and noisy. Let your older siblings or your neighbors spend the money to raise children who can then be taxed *to support you* in your old age." Those who listen become "free riders" on the system; but there is only reward, and no penalty, for this. Once again, the American social insurance scheme actually *tends to produce* the *problem* that it *assumed* at its beginning: low fertility.

Now, I am not the first person to notice this problem. Indeed, in his 1941 Godkin Lectures at Harvard University, the Swedish economist Gunnar Myrdal warned that America's new social security system had dangerously inverted the value of children: they were now a *burden* rather than an asset, a perverted result that would undermine the nation's very existence in the long run.[21] During the 1980s, Charles Hohm of the University of California, San Diego checked this "social security-fertility hypothesis" in a detailed study of nineteen developed and sixty-two underdeveloped nations. He found that "[a]fter controlling for relevant developmental effects, the level and scope of a country's Social Security program is causally and inversely related to fertility levels." Translated: higher benefits meant fewer children. Even the *reverse* hypothesis proved to be true: "Reduced fertility levels result in subsequent increases in Social Security expenditures," as the system devours itself.[22] This explains developments in Europe, where *depopulation, old age pensions*, and *tax burden* now advance in tandem.

More recently, economists Isaac Ehrlich and Francis T. Lui have shown that a pay-as-you-go old age security system "discourages families' incentives for self-reliance," drives fertility ever downward, reduces savings, and damages "investment in human capital," meaning children. These effects, according to Ehrlich and Lui, portend *both* social disintegration and "financial collapse."[23]

The Social Security system's fifth internal dilemma is the "efficiency contradiction." Even a cursory study of the nursing home industry reveals a tale of corruption, fraud, and abuse. The Family Research Council's President Kenneth Connor took the lead in exposing and fighting these problems in Florida during the 1990s. The curiosity, though, is how the fraud and abuse constantly reappear. Back in the 1960s, Mary Adelaide Mendelson's book, *Tender Loving Greed*, exposed the kickbacks that nursing home operators received from pharmacies and funeral homes, the frequent charges to government for non-delivered products and care, the maximum reimbursements claimed for patients needing minimum care, the lack of blankets, the starvation diets, the idle rehabilitation equipment, the cheap bread, the stolen meat, the fake water sprinklers, the filthy clothes, the deliberate withholding of soap and toilet paper, the outrageous "extra charges," the staff intimidation of some patients with others "drugged into oblivion," the fake diagnoses, the "gang visits" by physicians.[24] Regulatory reforms followed. A decade later, Bruce Vladeck's *Unloving Care: The Nursing Home Tragedy* chronicled a similar list of behaviors still endemic to the system. Regulatory reforms followed. In 1998, *Time* magazine reported on another epidemic of beatings, malnutrition, dehydration, and neglect to be found in Medicaid funded nursing care centers.[25] One of the nation's largest nursing home chains, Beverly Enterprises, pled guilty that same year to massive Medicaid fraud and received a fine of $175 million. The company's crimes included phony nurse sign-in sheets and fabricated medical-treatment records.[26] The Inspector General of the U.S. Department of Health and Human Services also warned in 1998 of a new kind of fraud devised by nursing homes and hospices, this time based on kickbacks for Medicare and Medicaid referrals for end-of-life care.[27] In recent years, California—to choose just one state—has seen a string of arrests and convictions for nursing home elder abuse, for the knowing hiring of "certified care givers" who had prior criminal convictions for assault, grand theft, and drug trafficking, and for the now familiar phony Medicaid claims.[28]

Why do we find this recurring tale of fraud and abuse in elder care? Some will cite the easy government money (indeed, back in the 1970s, word on Wall Street had it that "it is impossible to lose money" in the nursing home business). Others will point to inadequate regulation. I suggest that the real problem runs much deeper: namely, in the total failure of the "industrial model" when applied to the care of the very young *and* the very old.

The *industrial revolution* rested on a very few principles: specialization; the division of labor; standardized products. The system has worked miraculously well when the products are light bulbs and automobiles. But some Americans pushed the idea too far, into the care and nurture of human beings. Starting in the mid-nineteenth century, reformers took family-centered schooling and reorganized it on an industrial model: the massive public school system was born, itself operating as a kind of education factory. In the twentieth century, we saw a similar effort to industrialize the care of infants and toddlers (we call it "daycare") and *elder care*. The hope for the latter was that organizing the old in standardized beds and rooms to receive standardized care from specialists would generate gains of efficiency, and so of wealth. *But it does not work.* Human beings are not light bulbs or Dodge Caravans. Each person is unique and requires *personal* attention and care: the very opposite of what the industrial principle delivers. The recurring cases of fraud, neglect, and abuse in structured elder care, I suggest, derive from this misplaced quest for efficiency and profit *through services or actions that cannot—by their very nature—be successfully industrialized.* Put another way, the quest for "efficiency" and "profit" in the nursing home will *inevitably* produce neglect and abuse, because the quest itself in this locale is *dehumanizing*.

What, then, is to be done? Can we reform a structure that rewards institutionalization, penalizes altruism, discourages the multi-generational family, punishes childbearing, and auto-generates its own versions of abuse, fraud, and neglect? Rephrased positively, can we restore the familial bonds of the generations?

There are small steps or reforms that might be considered.

(1)   Some suggest that Medicare and Medicaid be altered to provide vouchers to persons (or their families) who might otherwise qualify for nursing home care. This voucher would expand family choices in the purchase of in-home assistance, adult daycare, respite care, foster care, and small group homes.[29] With limited exceptions, though, the use of

vouchers still involves primarily the purchase of services from outside vendors. While the nursing home might be avoided, this would do little to reconnect the members of a family.

(2)   A second option is to give *special tax incentives* to persons providing informal care to the elderly. Several states have experimented with this idea. Idaho has given a $1,000 tax deduction or a $100 credit to taxpayers who provided care to persons over age sixty-five. Arizona has offered taxpayers a $600 exemption if they have paid 25 percent or more of an elderly person's institutional or home health costs or at least $800 toward their general medical costs. In the first program, 80 percent of the caregivers turned out to be children of the elderly persons being helped. Three-quarters of the taxpayers in both states found the incentives to be of value as a support to continued family responsibility and care.[30] Federal tax deductions built on these principles and of similar or greater magnitude could have the same effect.

(3)   A third reform option would be to modify the law governing Child/ Elder Care Reimbursement Accounts (CECRA), available to employees at companies and organizations with "cafeteria benefit" plans. At present, this use of *pre-tax* dollars for elder care can *only* occur if the person is mentally and/or physically incapable of self-care *and* claimed as a dependent on the income tax. Changes could include loosening or discarding these restrictions and raising the cap on the pre-tax dollars available. Such measures would probably encourage more family-centered care.

(4)   A variation would be to grant a special tax break to a family with an elderly relative residing in its home. The Republican Party's 1999 tax plan proposed giving an extra personal exemption to households containing a relative over age sixty-five, even if not a dependent for taxation purposes.[31] In 2000, Democratic presidential candidate Al Gore proposed creating a federal tax credit of up to $3,000 for Americans providing long-term care to elderly relatives or friends.[32] In 2001, the New York State Senate considered a tax credit of 20 percent for expenses incurred through the care of an elderly relative living with the taxpayer, up to $3,000.[33]

(5)   A more sweeping idea is for Medicare and Medicaid simply to *hire* a family member as the caregiver for someone qualifying for public support, an idea already tried in France.[34] Susan Ettner proposes a variation on this, allowing insurers (including presumably Medicare and Medicaid) "to offer to pay informal caregivers (*at a lower rate*) to provide services for which the insurer would otherwise have to pay the home health agency."[35]

These are all worthy ideas. Combined into a package, they would predictably have a measurable positive effect.

And yet, at another level, they are still like band-aids over cancerous sores, slowing some of the bleeding but not tackling the disease.

Even with these reforms, the overarching system of social insurance would remain firmly in place. Its innate incentives against altruism, family care, and childbearing and in favor of institutionalization, abuse, and fraud would be only marginally contained.

What, then, about a "privatized" social insurance system? There are good arguments for the privatization of Social Security, some of which I have made myself.[36] In full candor, though, it is hard to see how any of the proposed privatization plans would, at this point, "restore the familial bonds of the generations." Indeed, most plans would probably inject a greater degree of individualism into the scheme. Still tied to earnings from outside work, privatized plans would do relatively little to encourage family-centered elder care, and could actually discourage it.

Authentic "intergenerational" reform requires that we enter the very heart of the system, and *rebuild incentives that truly favor both childbearing and family-centered elder care*. To do this, we first need to recognize that FICA "contributions" for OASDI and Medicare are, in fact, taxes, not insurance premiums. Most people now understand this and even some honest federal documents now label these extractions as taxes. Still, the implications of this reality are rarely drawn out. Next, we need to understand that the FICA tax is a full *15.3* percent on the labor of employed persons (that is, it includes both "employers" and "employees" portions). Third, we must remember that this regressive tax starts with the first hour of work. It is the very lifeblood of the Social Security system, and its negative effects fall most fully on young adults struggling to start families.

After these acknowledgements, an alternate and more sweeping series of reforms becomes fairly clear:

- First, taxpayers should be granted a credit of 20 percent against their total FICA tax for each child born or adopted, a credit to be continued until the child reaches age thirteen. This would mean that a family with five children, ages twelve and under, would pay no FICA tax in that year (but would still receive all due employment credit).
- Second, taxpayers should also be granted a 25 percent credit against their total FICA tax for each elderly parent or grandparent residing in the taxpayer's home.
- Third, for each child born, a mother should receive three years (or 12 quarters) of employment credits (calculated at the median fulltime income) toward her future Social Security pension.
- Fourth, a person should also receive one year's employment credit toward Social Security, at the same median income level, if he or she

served as the primary caregiver for an elderly relative residing in his or her home.

- And fifth, base FICA "contribution" rates could be raised to accommodate these reforms at a revenue-neutral level.
- *Or* the OASDI tax could be applied to *all* income and no longer capped off at incomes above $87,000 (in 2003).

Under this scheme, parenthood and family elder care would be encouraged rather than burdened and penalized. This reform would recognize that *new children*, rather than cash, are the real "contributions" that a social insurance system needs. It would take into account the cost-savings or *value* of intergenerational care as a favored substitute for institutional care. It would give motherhood a recognition as real work that is its due. And the intentionally childless would finally pay their fair share for social insurance.

Above all, we would—I believe—be rebuilding a fresh vision of the multigenerational family for a new American century.

Notes

1.   Robert F. Clark, "Home and Community-Based Care: The U.S. Example," *Canadian Journal on Aging* 15 (1996, Supplement 1): 91-102; and Brian Burwell, Mary Harahan, David Kennell, John Drabek, and Lisa Alecxin, "An Analysis of Long-Term Care Reform Proposals," a report prepared by Systemetrics, under contract with the U.S. Department of Health and Human Services, Office of Disability, Aging and Long-Term Care Policy, 1993; found at http://aspe.hhs.gov/daltcp/reports/reformes.htm.
2.   Found at: http://216.239.33.100/search?q=cache:x_BrXigOLdAC.
3.   Ralph Borsodi, *Education and Living* (New York: Devin-Adair, 1948): 413.
4.   Bruce C. Vladeck, *Unloving Care: The Nursing Home Tragedy* (New York: Basic Books, 1980): 34-35.
5.   W. Andrew Achenbaum, *Old Age in the New Land: The American Experience Since 1790* (Baltimore and London: The Johns Hopkins University Press, 1978): 127-28.
6.   *Report to the President of the Committee on Economic Security* (Washington, DC: U.S. Government Printing Office, 1935): 23-25.
7.   P. K. Whelpton, "Population: Trends in Differentials of True Increase and Age Composition," in *Social Changes in 1929*, ed. William F. Ogburn (Chicago: University of Chicago Press, 1930: 873-77).
8.   See: *Recent Social Trends in the United States: Report of the President's Research Committee on Social Trends* (New York: McGraw-Hill, 1933): 664-78.
9.   An influential article in this regard was: L. Hersh, "The Fall in the Birth Rate and its Effects on Social Policy," *International Labour Review* 28 (Aug. 1933): 159-62.
10. See: A. M. Rivlin, J. M. Weiner, R. J. Hanley, and D. A. Spence, *Caring for the Disabled Elderly: Who Will Pay?* (Washington, DC: The Brookings Institution, 1987).
11. Quotation from Vladeck, *Unloving Care*, p. 33.
12. Ibid., p. 242.

13. Mary Adelaide Mendelson and David Hapgood, "The Political Economy of Nursing Homes," *The Annals of the American Academy of Political and Social Science* 415 (Sept. 1974): 96.

14. See also: Ellen Schell, "The Origin of Geriatric Nursing: The Chronically Ill in Almhouses and Nursing Homes, 1900-1950," *Nursing History Review* 1 (1993): 203-16; and Muriel R. Gillick, "Long-Term Care Options for the Frail Elderly," *Journal of the American Geriatrics Society* 37 (Dec. 1989): 1201.

15. See: Bent Andersen, "Rationality and Irrationality of the Nordic Welfare State," *Daedalus* 113 (1984): 109-39.

16. Both Jackson, "Family Caregiving: Still Going Strong?" presentation at The Changing Face of Informal Caregiving, a conference sponsored by the Office of the Assistant Secretary for Planning and Evaluation, DHHS, Berkeley Springs, West Virginia, Oct. 15, 1992.

17. Vicki Ann Freedman, "Averting Nursing Home Care: The Role of Family Structure," doctoral dissertation, Yale University, 1993.

18. Burwell, "An Analysis of Long-Term Care Reform Proposals," p. 3.

19. Ibid., p. 9.

20. Susan L. Ettner, "The Effect of The Medicaid Home Care Benefit on Long-Term Care Choices of the Elderly," *Economic Inquiry* 32 (Jan. 1994): 105.

21. See: Gunnar Myrdal, *Population: A Problem for Democracy* (Cambridge, MA: Harvard University Press, 1942).

22. Charles F. Hohm et al., "A Reappraisal of the Social Security-Fertility Hypothesis: A Bidirectional Approach," *The Social Science Journal* 23 (1986): 149-68.

23. Isaac Ehrlich and Frances T. Lui, "Social Security, The Family, and Economic Growth," *Economic Inquiry* 36 (July 1998): 390-409.

24. Mendelson, *Tender Loving Greed*, pp. 3-29.

25. "Shining a Light on Abuse," Time.com: http://www.time.com/time/magazine/1998/dom/980803/nation.shining_a_light_06.html.

26. "Nursing Home Chain Hit with Record Medicare Fraud Fine," U.S. Law.com, http://www.uslaw.com/library/article/???NursingHome.html?area_id=17.

27. Office of Inspector General, "Special Fraud Alert: Fraud and Abuse in Nursing Home Arrangements with Hospices," U.S. Department of Health and Human Services, March 1998.

28. "Attorney General Lockyer Announces Arrest of 21 to Break Up Alleged Elder Care Fraud Ring," at http://caag.state.ca.us/bmfea/press/01-048.htm; "Attorney General Lockyer Announces Criminal Convictions of Nursing Home Administrator," at http://caag.state.ca.us/bmfea/press/02-041.htm; and "Grand Jury Indicts Nursing Home and its Owner of Fraud," *Business Journal* (San Jose), May 7, 2001.

29. See, for example, James L. Wilkes II, "Building a Better Long-Term Care System: The Potential of Community-Based Care," *Family Policy* 14 (July/Aug. 2001): 14.

30. See: M. C. Hendrickson, "State Tax Incentives for Persons Giving Informal Care to the Elderly," *Health Care Financing Review: Annual Supplement* (1998): 123-28.

31. Curt Anderson, "GOP Tax Bill Helps with Elder Care," Associated Press, July 24, 1999; at http://www.apeape.org/goptax.html.

32. "Gore Would Help Families and Friends Meet Long-Term Care Needs of Loved Ones," Gore Campaign Release, June 7, 2000; at: http://www.taxplanet.com/library/gorelongtermcare/gorelongtermcare.html.

33. "Senate Proposes $65 Million Elder Care Tax Credit," New York State Senate, March 13, 2001; at: http://www.senate.ny.us.

34. "Gender Issues in Care for the Dependent Elderly," *CNRS-Info* (No. 398-Dec. 2001) at: http://www.cnrs.fr/Cnrspresse/n398/html/en398a04.htm.

35. Ettner, "The Effect of the Medicaid Home Care Benefit on Long-Term Care Choices of the Elderly," p. 125.
36. Allan Carlson, "Personal Savings Accounts Would Strengthen Families," *The American Enterprise* 8 (Jan./Feb. 1997): 58-59.

Appendix

An American Family Policy for the Twenty-First Century

Regarding Marriage:

- The states should reintroduce "fault" into their laws governing divorce. "Covenant marriage" measures, which create a voluntarily entered, higher-tiered marriage requiring a finding of fault for dissolution, are a relatively painless way to start the process. Ideally, fault would be introduced in divorce law across the board, to underscore the communal nature of marriage and the social gravity of divorce.
- All governments should treat marriage as a full economic partnership. At the federal level, this would mean reintroducing full "income splitting" in the federal income tax, as existed between 1948 and 1963. Such a measure would eliminate the most notorious "marriage penalty." At the state level, this principle would encourage broad application of the "community property" concept inherited from the old Hispanic law codes of the American Southwest.
- The legal status of marriage, and any benefits and obligations that it confers, should be restricted to the monogamous bonds of women to men, because this is from where children come. Ideally, this ancient principle would continue to be recognized by courts and lawmakers in the fifty states. Recent judicial actions, though, point to the need for an amendment to the U.S. Constitution to protect marriage, as so defined. This amendment would serve as a shield to protect the marital bond—the primal base of the family—from judicially imposed social engineering. In deference to the principle of liberty, other human friendships and relationships are properly left unregulated and unregistered.
- It is appropriate for federal and state public welfare programs, such as Temporary Assistance to Needy Families (TANF) grants, to seek ways to encourage and affirm marriage among aid recipients. The public interest is deeply involved in the state of marriage. Indeed, marriage is the quickest path out of poverty and public dependency for welfare recipients. The federal government can play here an affirmative role.

135

Regarding Birth or Population Policy:

- The president of the United States should formally repudiate National Security Staff Memorandum #200 *and* the 1972 Report of the Commission on Population Growth and the American Future. They are deeply flawed, scientifically untenable, misleading, and irrelevant.
- An American administration should articulate new principles for a twenty-first-century population policy, ones to be applied both at home and abroad:

  - ➤ The United States of America holds the family to be the fundamental social unit, inscribed in human nature, and centered on the voluntary union of a man and a woman in a covenant of marriage for the purposes of propagating and rearing children, sharing intimacy and resources, and conserving lineage and tradition.
  - ➤ The USA recognizes that strong families commonly rest on religiously grounded morality systems, which deserve autonomy and respect as vital aspects of civil society.
  - ➤ The USA views large families, created responsibly through marriage, as special gifts to their societies, deserving affirmation and encouragement.
  - ➤ The USA recognizes that social, cultural, and economic progress depends on the renewal of human population. Population growth is in the nation's best interest.
  - ➤ And the USA underscores that the demographic problem facing the twenty-first century is depopulation, not overpopulation.

- Relative to domestic policy, these principles point toward:

  - ➤ A doubling of the real value of the personal income tax exemption for children (currently $3,000 per child) and the child tax credit (currently $1,000 per child under age sixteen) and the elimination of income-based restrictions on their availability.
  - ➤ The repeal of Title X of the Public Health Services Act, which subsidizes over 4000 birth control clinics across the nation. Crafted during the "overpopulation" hysteria of the late 1960s, Title X discourages fertility of all kinds, including within marriage, encourages sexual hedonism, subverts parental responsibility, and purposefully targets teenagers and minorities for conversion to an anti-natalist culture. In sum, it encourages the very attitudes and behaviors that create the "depopulation" problem.

- Relative to foreign policy, these principles point toward the rechanneling of all American aid programs away from "reproductive" or "family planning" services and toward family building strategies. American funds should be restricted to:

> ➤ Abstinence education projects, premised on chastity before marriage and fidelity within;
> ➤ Marriage promotion initiatives;
> ➤ Maternal and child health projects, designed to save infant lives and safeguard future childbearing;
> ➤ And economic development projects that respect and encourage family autonomy and initiative.

Regarding Infant and Toddler Care:

• Replace the existing Dependent Care Tax Credit with a universal tax credit of $2,500 per child, ages birth to five. This credit would be available to all parents of preschoolers, both those with a parent full time at home and those purchasing substitute care. It should be refundable to those parents without the income to claim the full credit, allowing for a reduction in means-tested government daycare subsidies. The value of the credit should also be indexed to inflation.
• Corporate tax deductions and credits for maintaining daycare centers should be phased out.

Regarding the Education of the Young:

• Home education should be protected. The states should reform their compulsory education laws along the model of Alaska, where any child is exempted who "is being educated in the child's home by a parent or legal guardian." This law precludes registration, reporting, or curricular requirements.
• Educational diversity should be encouraged in ways that reinforce family autonomy and school independence. "Tuition tax credits" are too narrow in their focus, giving no recognition to home-educating families. "Vouchers" tend to make private and religious schools dependent on state funds, open these institutions to potential regulation, and subtly erode the virtues of personal and familial sacrifice that are key to the success of independent schools.

Instead:

> ➤ Per capita child tax deductions and credits, without any link to schooling, should be preferred at both the state and federal levels; and
> ➤ New tax credits on *all* forms of educational expense (including books, fees, tuition, and special lessons) should be created, with the Illinois law (allowing a credit of 20 percent on such expenses up to $500) as the model; *or*

> ➤ *All* educational expenses (from preschool fees and home schooling expenses to university tuition) could be treated as an investment in *human capital*, logically enjoying full income tax deductability.

• To restore educational liberty and neighborhood integrity, all public school systems should be deconsolidated to single-school districts. Each neighborhood or township school would have its own elected governing board and its own tax levy. Where the economic circumstances of a school district were inadequate, a state education board could provide a supplemental grant out of general revenues. High school districts could draw students from several independent primary districts. These public schools, moreover, would be "open." Like a community college, they would offer their learning and extra-curricula opportunities to all families in the district, but would compel none. Some might choose a complete school day; others just a class or two; still others only participation on a sports team. These schools would again be able to reflect the values of local communities and would have strong incentives to *serve* the neighborhood and its inhabitants.

Regarding Suburbia as "Home" to the Nation:

• The need is to refunctionalize individual homes, abandoning governmental biases toward the frail "companionate model" of family home-design and opening suburban life to a return of the "productive home." Specific regulatory reforms would include:

> ➤ At the federal level, abolishing FHA and other public underwriting rules that discourage the creation of home offices, home schools, and home businesses;
> ➤ At the state level, ending those regulations of the professions—such as medicine, law, dentistry, and accounting—that favor giant institutions and prohibit decentralized learning such as apprenticeships; standardized exams alone should determine competence and licensing;
> ➤ At the local level, loosening or abolishing zoning laws to allow the flourishing of home gardens, modest animal husbandry, home offices and businesses, and home schools; in place of zoning, the more flexible "nuisance laws" of the early twentieth century should be restored as guardians of neighborhood tranquility;
> ➤ At the neighborhood or "development" level, loosening in whatever manner possible "restrictive covenants" that coerce families into the failed "companionship" life model; Homeowners Associations in new developments should be discouraged.

Regarding the Taxation of Families:

- The Spirit of '48 should be restored by the return of pure "income splitting" (see Marriage), the doubling of the Dependent Exemption for children (see Birth), and the doubling of the Child Tax Credit (see Birth again).
- If Congress ever moves toward a "flat" income tax, there should be a universal per capita exemption of at least $10,000 per family member, indexed to inflation.
- If Congress ever decides on a more radical shift, from an "income" tax to a "consumption" tax, the family's interests should be protected by a generous *per capita* rebate designed to shield basic family consumption.

Regarding the Home Economy:

- Intentional family-centered communities should be encouraged, most certainly including those bound by religious conviction. Relative to public policy, the primary need is to protect community autonomy from overzealous state authorities.

Regarding Elder Care and the Bonds of the Generations:

- The current system discourages both the birth of children and family care of the frail elderly.
- Modest reforms might be considered:
  - ➢ Medicare and Medicaid could be altered to provide vouchers to persons (or families) who might otherwise qualify for nursing home care;
  - ➢ Special federal or state tax incentives could be given to persons providing informal care to the elderly;
  - ➢ The law governing Child/Elder Care Reimbursement Accounts (CECRA) could be modified to loosen existing limits on elder care (currently, the care recipient must be mentally or physically incapable of self care and claimed as a dependent on this income tax);
  - ➢ Special tax benefits (such as a tax credit of up to $3,000) could be provided to a family with an elderly relative residing in its home; and
  - ➢ Medicare or Medicaid could hire a family member as the caregiver, at a somewhat lower rate, for someone qualifying for public support.
- True "intergenerational" reform would rebuild incentives that favor both childbearing and family-centered elder care, by restructuring incentives within the Medicare and Social Security systems:

➤ Taxpayers should be granted a credit of 20 percent against their total FICA (payroll) tax for each child born or adopted, a credit to be continued until the child reaches age thirteen. This would mean that a family with five children, ages twelve and under, would pay no FICA tax in that year (but would still receive all due employment credit);

➤ Taxpayers should be granted a 25 percent credit against their total FICA tax for each elderly parent or grandparent residing in the taxpayer's home;

➤ For each child born, a mother should receive three years (12 quarters) of employment credits (calculated at the median fulltime income) toward her future Social Security pension;

➤ A person should also receive one year's employment credit toward Social Security, at the same median income level, if he or she served as the primary caregiver for an elderly relative residing in his or her home; and

➤ Base FICA tax rates could be raised to accommodate these reforms at a revenue-neutral level (so shifting the tax burden onto those without children and/or refusing to care for their own); or the OASDI tax could be applied to all income and no longer capped off at incomes over $87,000 (in 2003).

Index

Achenbaum, W. Andrew, 120
African Americans, Civil Rights Act and, 112-113
Aid to Families with Dependent Children, 49
Alliance for Marriage, 2
American Council of Life Insurers, 119
American Law Institute, 2
Aries, Philippe, 26
Ayres, L. P., 59

Bailey, Dean, 60
Bailey, Liberty Hyde, 60
Bales, Alba, 61
Becker, Gary, 20, 110
Berry, Wendell, 9-10, 64, 114
Bittker, Boris, 100
Borsodi, Ralph, 120
Boskin, Michael J., 95
Bouma-Prediger, Steven, 64
Brigham Young University, 6
Brogan, Dennis, 77-78
Burgess, Ernest, 39, 110
Bush, President George W., 101
Business Week, 10

Caldwell, John C., 22, 58
Chamie, Joseph, 19
Chesterton, G. K., 10-11, 109
Childcare
    collective childcare as, 37-38
    experimental centers for, 40
    industrial child rearing, 38-39
    progressive sociology and, 39-40
    women's liberation and, 36-37
Christensen, Bryce, 64
Civil Rights Act
    African American treatment and, 112-113
    school reverse segregation, 68
Coleman, David, 25

Common School Journal, 57, 64
Common schools, family displaying by, 56-58
Connor, Kenneth, 127
Coontz, Stephanie, 73

Davis, Kingsley, 7
Daycare centers
    American agenda for, 47-48
    as class exploitation, 50-51
    creating of, 43
    health risk of, 50
    Sweden's debates over, 47
    tax relief for, 96-97
    worker training for, 44
de Bonald, Louis, 4
de Tocqueville, Alexis, 5
Depopulation
    Asia and, 19
    environmental impacts from, 19
    reality of, 18-19
    U.S. policy and, 17-18
    world fertility declining, 18
Dewey, John, 57
Divorce, 10

Ehrlich, Isaac, 126-127
Ehrlich, Paul, 95
Eisenhower, President Dwight, 112
Engles, Friedrich, 36
European Fertility Project, 21

Family economies
    advertising influences on, 109
    Civil Rights Act and, 112-113
    counterattacking industrialization, 110
    economic logic strategies, 114-116
    family institutionalizing, 108-109
    family size manipulating, 112
    family system crisis, 111-112
    family wage system, 110-111